W9-DDD-891

Paul

Cézanne

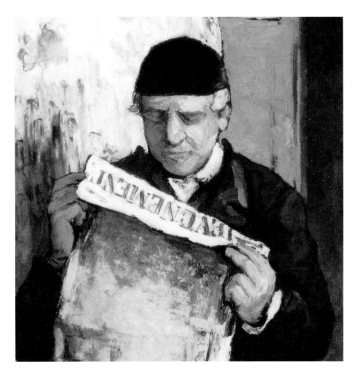

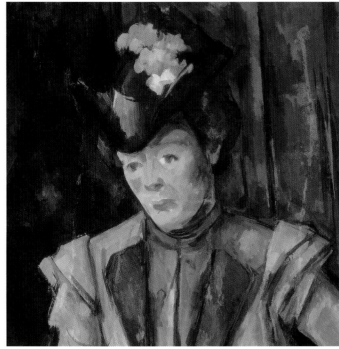

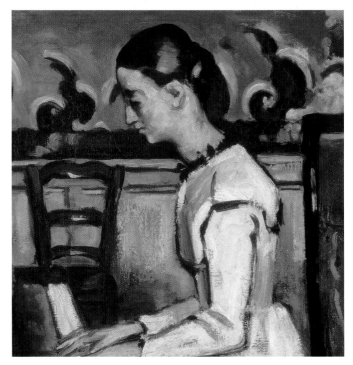

Cover: Stéphanie Angoh
Page layout: Julien Depaulis

© Confidential Concepts, worldwide, USA, 2003
© Sirocco, London, 2003 (English version)

Published in 2003 by Grange Books
an imprint of Grange Books Plc
The Grange Kingsnorth Industrial Estate
Hoo, nr Rochester Kent ME3 9ND
www.Grangebooks.co.uk
ISBN 1-84013-555-7

All rights reserved. No part of this publication may be
reproduced or adapted without the permission of the
copyright holder, throughout the world. Unless otherwise
specified, copyright on the works reproduced lies with the
respective photographers. Despite intensive research, it has
not always been possible to establish copyright ownership.
Where this is the case we would appreciate notification.

Paul

Cézanne

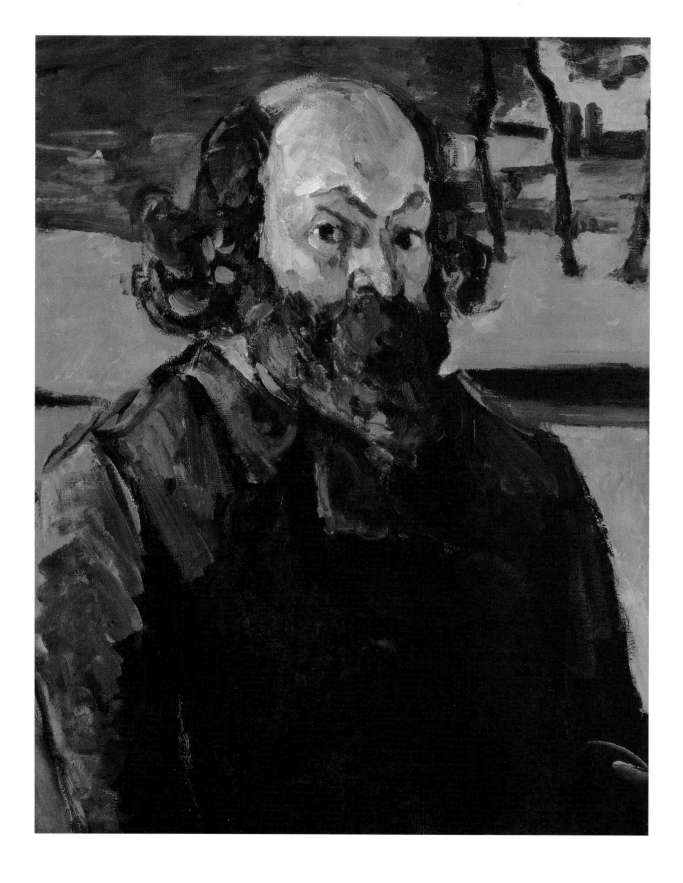

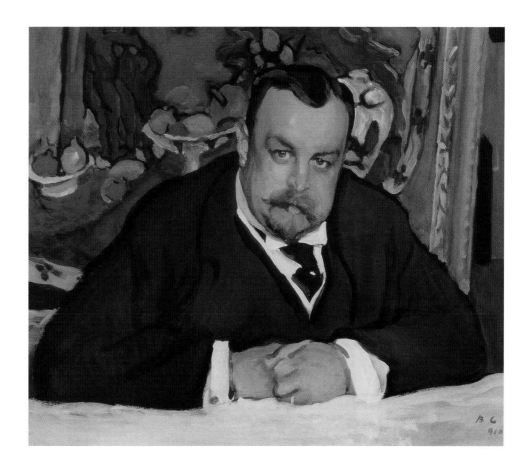

At the turn of the century, Cézanne began to be taken more and more seriously by the avant-garde: Matisse, Picasso, Braque, Vlaminck, Derain, and others, among them young Russian painters whose new art owed much to the master from Provence. However, many of Cézanne's contemporaries did not realize his true greatness. When Paul Cézanne died in October 1906 in Aix-en-Provence, the Paris newspapers reacted by publishing a handful of rather equivocal obituaries. "Imperfect talent," "crude painting," "an artist that never was," "incapable of anything but sketches," owing to "a congenital sight defect" — such were the epithets showered on the great artist during his lifetime and repeated at his graveside.

This was not merely due to a lack of understanding on the part of individual artists and critics, but above all to an objective factor — the complexity of his art, his specific artistic system which he developed throughout his career and did not embody *in toto* in any single one of his works. Cézanne was perhaps the most complex artist of the nineteenth century.

1. *Portrait of the Artist*, ca. 1873-1876. Musée d'Orsay, Paris.

2. *Portrait of Ivan Morozov*.

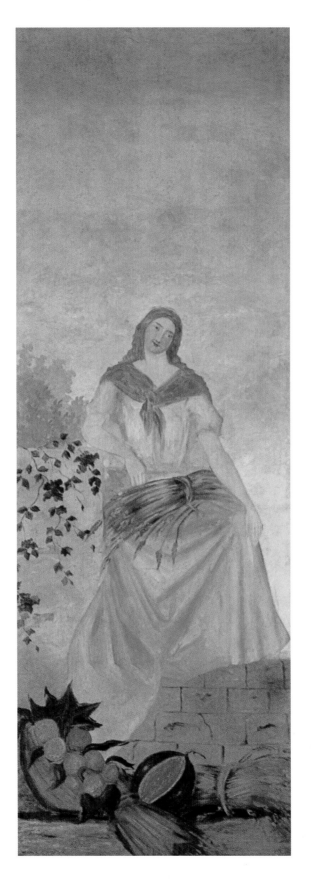
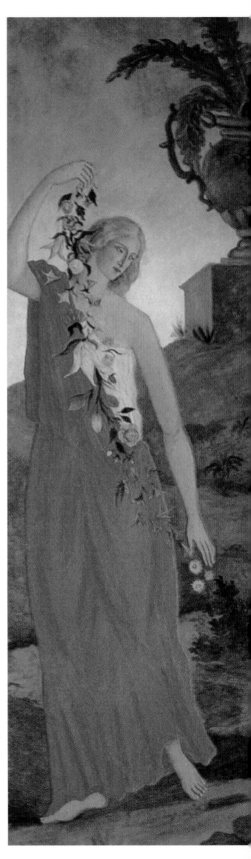

3. *The Four Seasons*,
1859-1860. Musée du
Petit Palais, Paris.

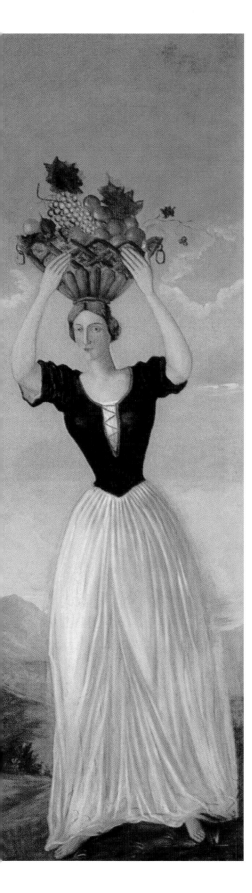
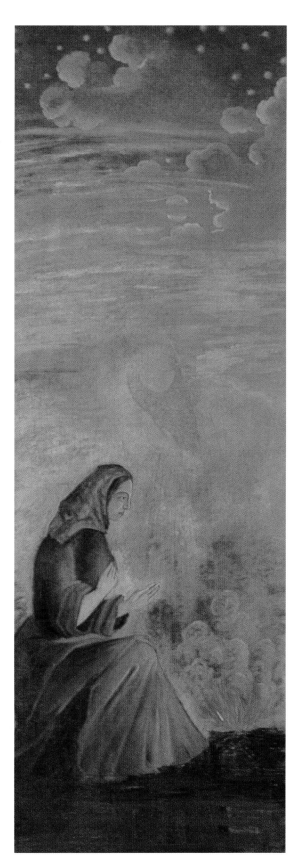

"One cannot help feeling something akin to awe in the face of Cézanne's greatness," wrote Lionello Venturi. "You seem to be entering an unfamiliar world — rich and austere with peaks so high that they seem inaccessible."[1] It is not in fact an easy thing to attain those heights.

Today Cézanne's art unfolds before us with all the consistency of a logical development, the first stages of which already contain the seeds of the final fruit. But to a person who could see only separate fragments of the whole, much of Cézanne's œuvre must naturally have seemed strange and incomprehensible. Most people were struck by the odd diversity of styles and the differing stages of completion of his paintings.
In some paintings, one saw a fury of emotion, which bursts through in vigorous, tumultuous forms and in brutally powerful volumes apparently sculpted in colored clay; in others, there was rational, carefully conceived composition and an incredible variety of color modulations. Some works resembled rough sketches in which a few transparent brushstrokes produced a sense of depth, while in others, powerfully modeled figures entered into complex, interdependent spatial relationships — what the Russian artist Alexei Nürenberg has aptly called "the tying together of space."[2]
Cézanne himself, with his constant laments about the impossibility of conveying his own sensations, prompted critics to speak of the fragmentary character of his work. He saw each of his paintings as nothing but an incomplete part of the whole.
Often, after dozens of interminable sessions, Cézanne would abandon the picture he had started, hoping to return to it later. In each succeeding work he would try to overcome the imperfection of the previous one, to make it more finished than before: "I am long on hair and beard but short on talent."[3] Exactly a month before his death, Cézanne wrote to Émile Bernard: "Shall I attain the aim so ardently desired and so long pursued?
I want to, but as long as the goal is not reached, I shall feel a vague malaise until I reach the haven, that is, until I achieve a greater perfection than before, and thus prove the tightness of my theories."

Such thoughts, shot through with bitterness, are a tragic theme recurring in Cézanne's correspondence and conversations with his friends. They are the tragedy of his whole life — a tragedy of constant doubting, dissatisfaction, and lack of confidence in his own ability. But here, too, was the mainspring of his art, which developed as a tree grows or a rock forms — by the slow accumulation of more and more new layers on a given foundation.

4. *Two Women and Child in an Interior*, early 1860s. The Pushkin Museum of Fine Arts, Moscow.

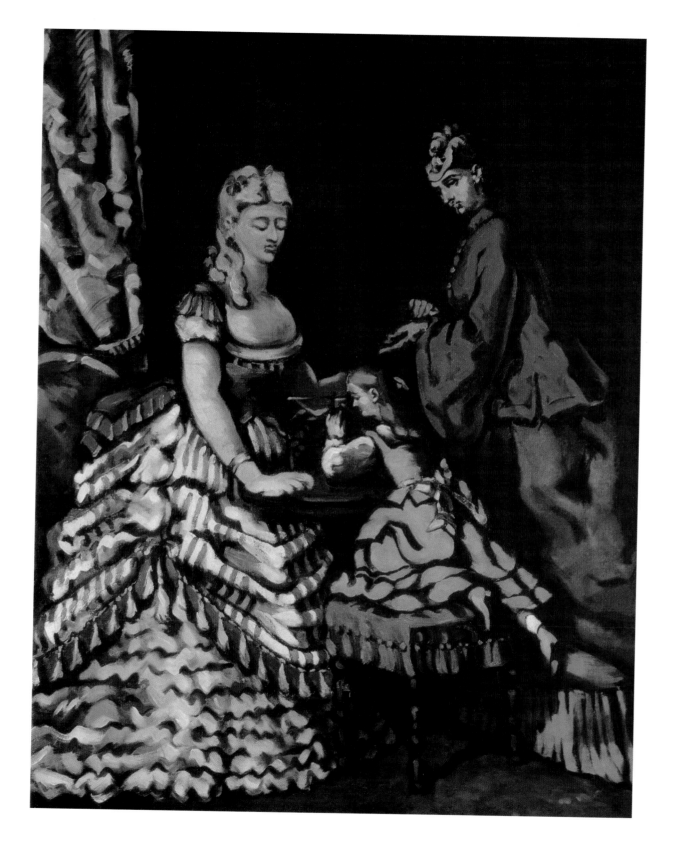

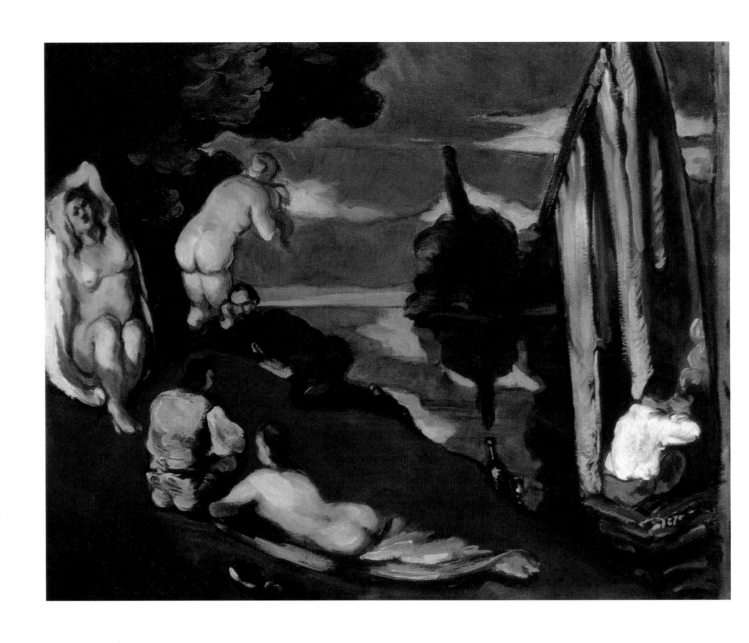

5. *Pastoral*, ca. 1870.
   Musée d'Orsay, Paris.

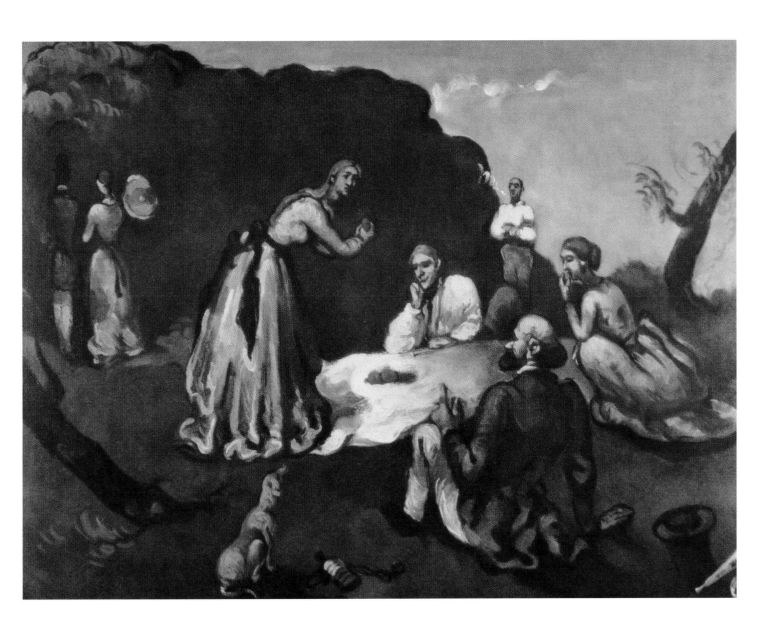

6. *Luncheon on the Grass*, ca. 1870-1871. Private Collection, Paris.

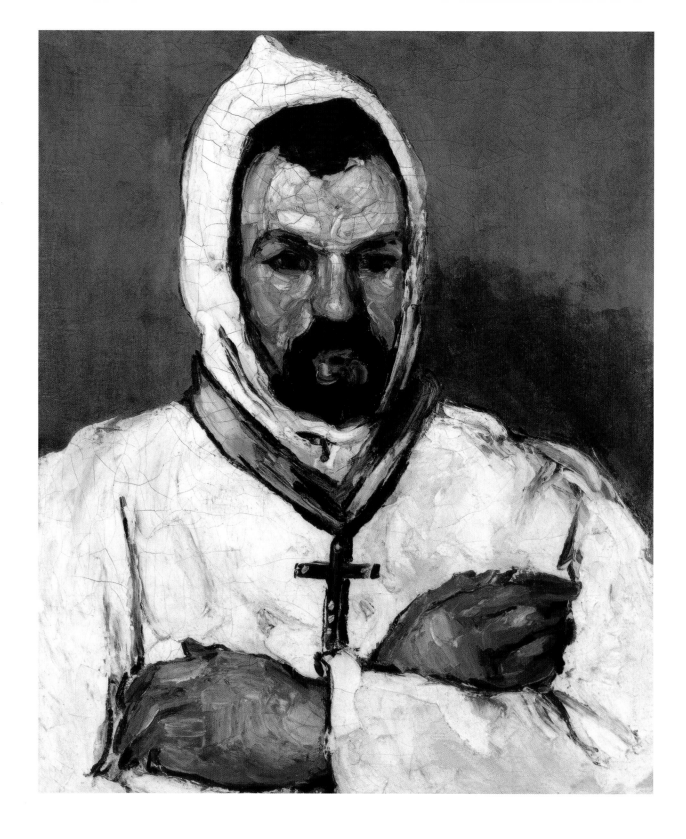

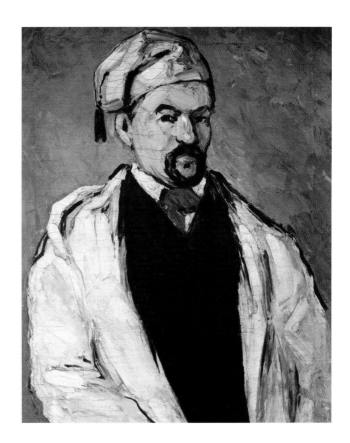

Often Cézanne would take a knife and scrape off all he had managed to paint during a day of hard work, or in a fit of exasperation throw it out of the window. He was also prone, when moving from one studio to another, to forget to take with him dozens of paintings he considered unfinished. He hoped eventually to render his entire vision of the world in one great, complete work of art, as did the geniuses of classical painting, and having "redone Nature according to Poussin," to emulate Poussin.[4] But to a person living at the end of the nineteenth century the surrounding reality seemed far more complex and unstable than to someone living in Poussin's time.

Cézanne devoted many years to the search for such means, hoping eventually to bring them all together. His ultimate aim was to paint a masterpiece, and he did create many works that we now consider to be masterpieces. But apart from that, he evolved a new creative method and a new artistic system which he adhered to consistently throughout his life. In creating this system he contributed to the birth of twentieth-century art. It would be useless to look for the essence and meaning of Cézanne's new artistic system in his own pronouncements. Cézanne had no use for thoughts on art expressed by any other means except "with brush in hand."

7. *Portrait of Uncle Dominic as a Monk*, ca. 1865. Mr and Mrs Ira Haupt Collection, New York.

8. *The Man with a Cotton Cap* (*Uncle Dominic*), 1865. The Museum of Modern Art, New York.

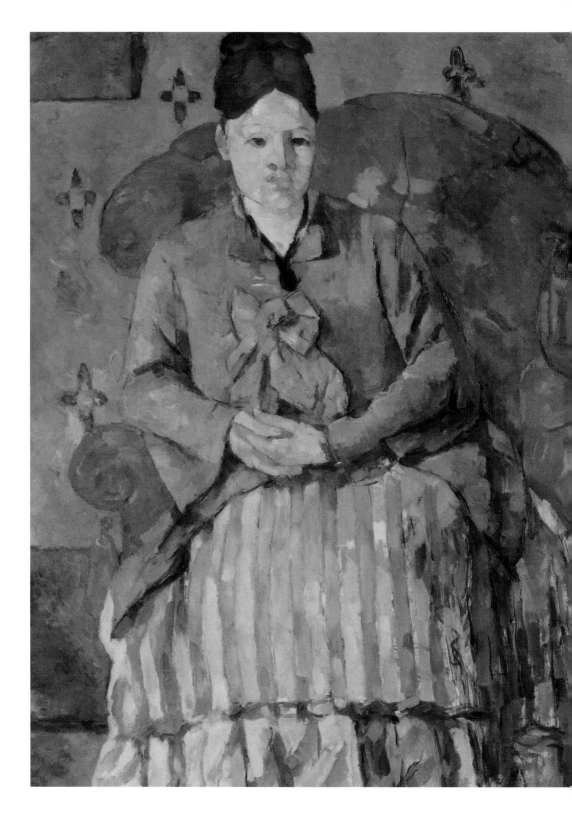

9. *Madame Cézanne in
a Red Armchair*,
1877. Museum of
Fine Arts, Boston.

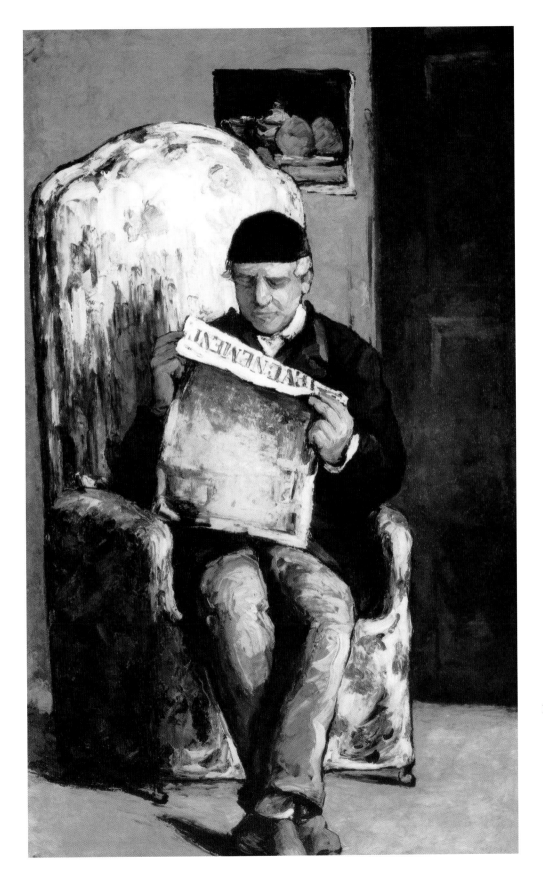

10. *Portrait of Louis*
 Auguste Cézanne,
 (The Artist's Father).
 1866-1867. Museum
 of Art, Saint-Louis.

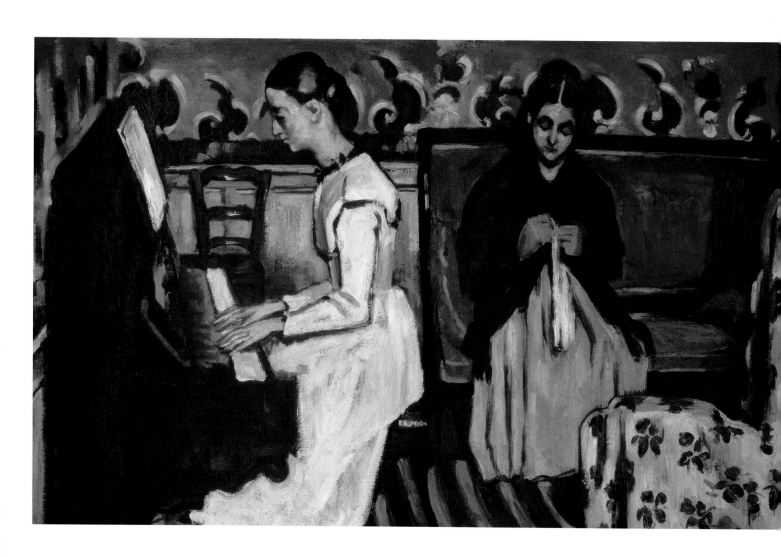

11. ***Girl at the Piano***
(*Overture to
'Tannhäuser'*),
1868–1869.
The Hermitage
Museum,
Saint-Petersburg.

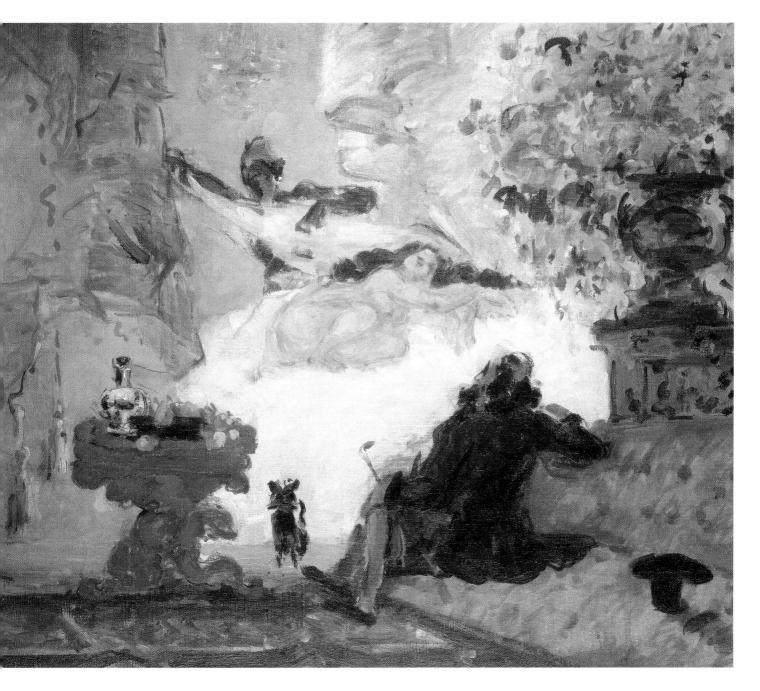

12. *Modern Olympia*, ca.
1873. Musée d'Orsay,
Paris.

His pronouncements bear the stamp not so much of theoretical postulates as of practical advice to fellow artists. It is not therefore to the artist's theoretical statements but to his works that we must look for an explanation of how his creative method gradually came into its own, how the links of the whole chain which today we justly call "Cézanne's artistic system" were forged.

In April 1861, the 22-year-old Paul Cézanne, son of a wealthy banker in Aix-en-Provence, arrived in Paris. His aim, his passion, his most fervent wish was to devote himself body and soul to art. Behind him was a solid classical education received in the college of Aix, rather modest successes (according to his teachers) at the local school of drawing and, above all, years of rapturous absorption of the unrestrained romanticism of Victor Hugo, Alfred de Musset, and Charles Baudelaire, years of youthful dreaming, together with Émile Zola, of the lofty calling of the artist and of their future collaboration in the field of art.

In his first year in Paris, Cézanne evidently still had a certain respect for the acknowledged masters and was willing to join them. During this short period he was at a crossroads; being not fully aware of his talent, he was trying in vain to find himself, and finally returned to Aix, acceding to his father's wishes, to continue the family business. One day he wrote on a page in a ledger:

Mon père le banquier ne voit pas sans frémir,
Au fond de son comptoir naître un peintre à venir…

Ultimately Cézanne the banker was obliged to abandon his hopes of making his son a worthy successor to himself in business; granting him a very modest allowance of 250 francs a month, he let Paul go to Paris to devote himself to his consuming passion. There Cézanne took up art in earnest. Anxious to obtain a fundamental artistic training, he was preparing to enter the École des Beaux-Arts and worked hard at the Academie Suisse in a desire to improve his technique. He failed the entrance examination for the École des Beaux-Arts, but at the same time found new friends, above all Camille Pissarro, who was to exert a substantial influence on his artistic development.

During that first decade, generally considered from the years 1859 to 1870, Cézanne's work was marked by a wealth of themes and experiments. Among the few surviving works of his youth are genre scenes, compositions on religious and mythological subjects, and decorative allegoric panels with which he adorned the walls of the Jas de Bouffan, his parents' estate. Sometimes these are copies of prints or of pictures from his mother's and sister's fashion magazines.

13. **Road at Pontoise**
(*Clos des Mathurins*),
1875–1877.
The Pushkin Museum
of Fine Arts, Moscow.

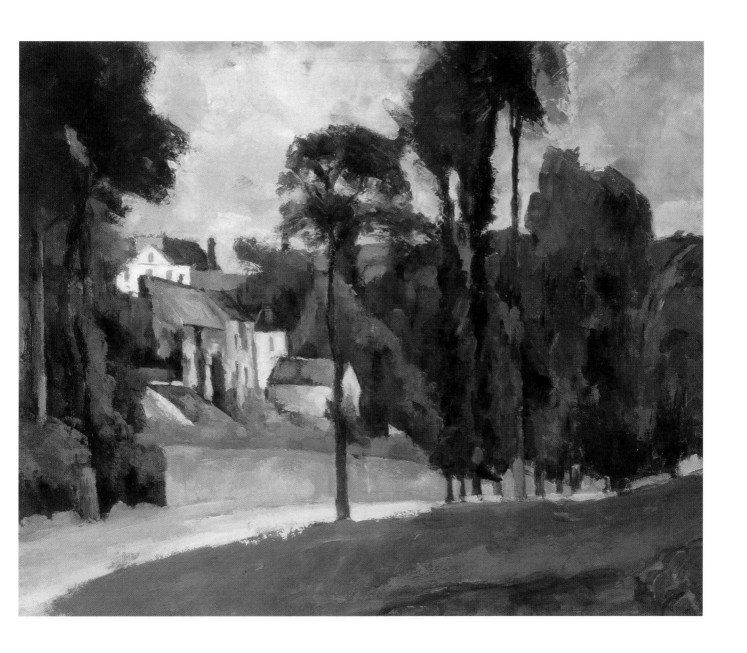

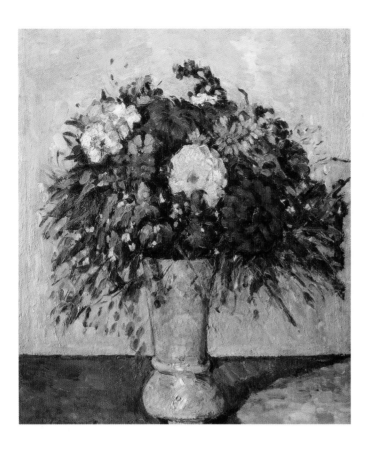

14. *Flowers in a Blue Vase*, 1873–1875. The Hermitage Museum, Saint Petersburg.

15. *Self-Portrait with a Cap*, 1873–1875. The Hermitage Museum, Saint Petersburg.

These early works already bear the stamp of the artist's individuality. They reveal his love for powerful, massive forms and simplified light-and-shade relations.

He was in no hurry to follow the Impressionists out of the museum halls and the studio's atmosphere of concentration in order to paint in the open air. He was immersed in an imaginary fantasy world, consumed by the desire to express an irresistible flood of human passion. Then, as before, he was attracted, above all, by the art of strong emotions. For an artist with Cézanne's keen sense of the dramatic complexity of the world, a simple representation of the visible was insufficient. He would constantly modify and deform figures, emphasizing in them what he thought to be most important and creating compositions with unstable equilibrium.

Two Women and Child in an Interior (*Scène d'intérieur*) (Pushkin Museum of Fine Arts)(p.9), the earliest of Cézanne's pictures in Russian museums, was executed in the 1860s. Cézanne achieves an effect of depth by the use of a few skillfully arranged objects: a curtain, a small table, and an armchair. The figures of two women and a girl are grouped around a goldfish bowl.

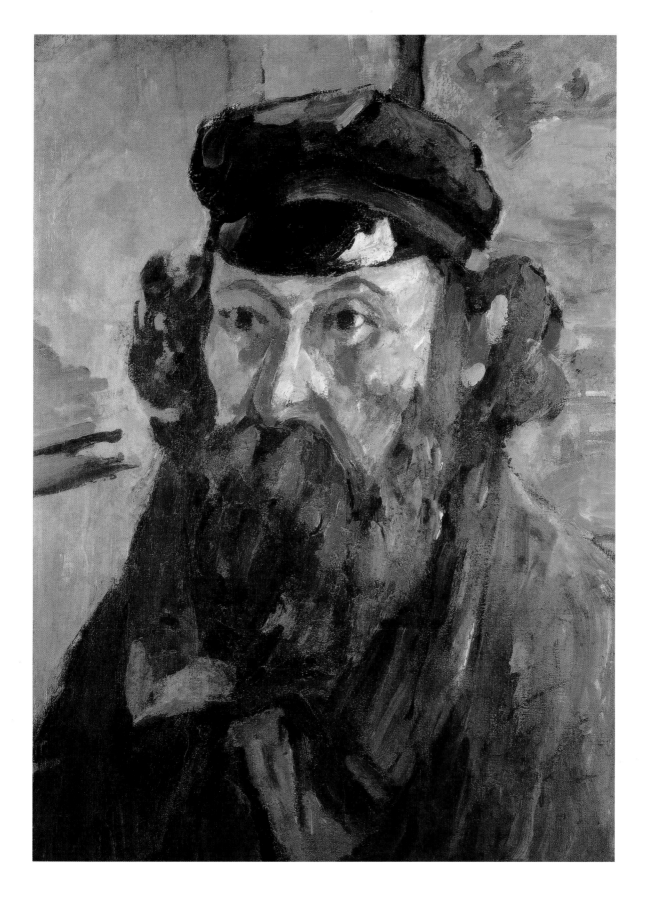

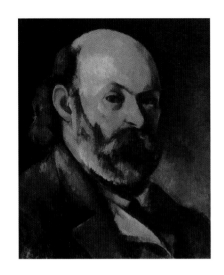

16. *Self-Portrait*,
1879-1885.
The Pushkin Museum
of Fine Arts, Moscow.

Their poses are thematically not defined, their movements slow, they are absorbed in themselves as if spellbound by the measured movements of the three goldfish in the water. The same dull, dark tone is used for the background, the deep shadows on the objects, and the water in the goldfish bowl. And this creates a sense of one environment, enclosing human beings, fish and objects alike. A hypnotizing atmosphere of inner concentration pervades the scene, mutes the sonority of the colors, and slows down the characters' movements, transforming what is in essence an ordinary genre scene into a kind of fantastic dream.

The inner tension, still bound by static forms in *Two Women and Child in an Interior*, is released with tremendous explosive force in other paintings, accompanied by a buildup of color contrasts. Traditional subjects like *Pastoral (p.10)*, *Luncheon on the Grass (p.11)*, *Fishing*, and others are set in unreal, fantastic surroundings reminiscent of strange, dreamlike visions.

The painting *The Murder* (1867–70, Walker Art Gallery, Liverpool)(p.24) seems to be seen through the eyes of a man stunned by the sight of the murderer's hand raised over his victim. Forms here are generalized in the extreme and are subordinated to a whirlwind of movement: the man's clothes rise corkscrew fashion following the thrust of the hand clutching the knife; on the right there emerges from the depth a sinister female figure, a kind of chimera, the whole weight of her boulder-like body falling upon the victim; the sharply designated diagonal of the landscape plane recedes into the depths of the painting, and a swirling storm-cloud hangs low over the scene. Cézanne put a lot of effort into this composition, as is evidenced by the large number of preparatory drawings. Yet it still looks as if it were painted in a transport of frenzy — the artist applied thick dabs of paint with a palette knife and modeled form with pools of color, striving to truthfully express his own powerful sensations.

These works were born in the heated imagination of a painter living in provincial bourgeois surroundings, where everything was in opposition to his strivings and hostile to the urgings of his rather prolonged youth. He took up with Hortense Fiquet, a girl not of his social class, but for many years — until 1886, when he turned forty — he was obliged to conceal the liaison and the birth of his son from his father, and to live and keep his family on an irregular pittance.

Cézanne's *Orgy* (1864–68, private collection, Paris), *Pastoral* (c. 1870, ex- collection of J. Pellerin, Paris), *Luncheon on the Grass* (1869–70, private collection, Paris), and many other works painted in the late sixties and early seventies, are permeated with an atmosphere of unreality.

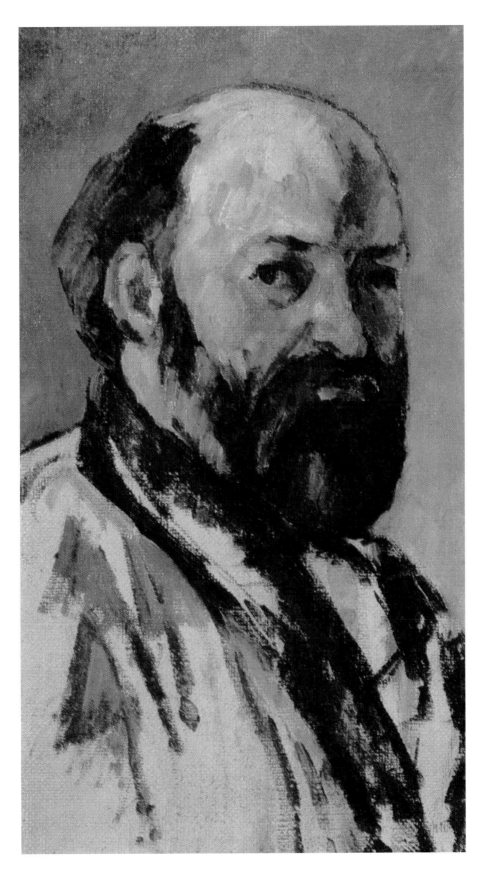

17. *Self-Portrait*,
   1880-1881.
   Musée d'Orsay, Paris.

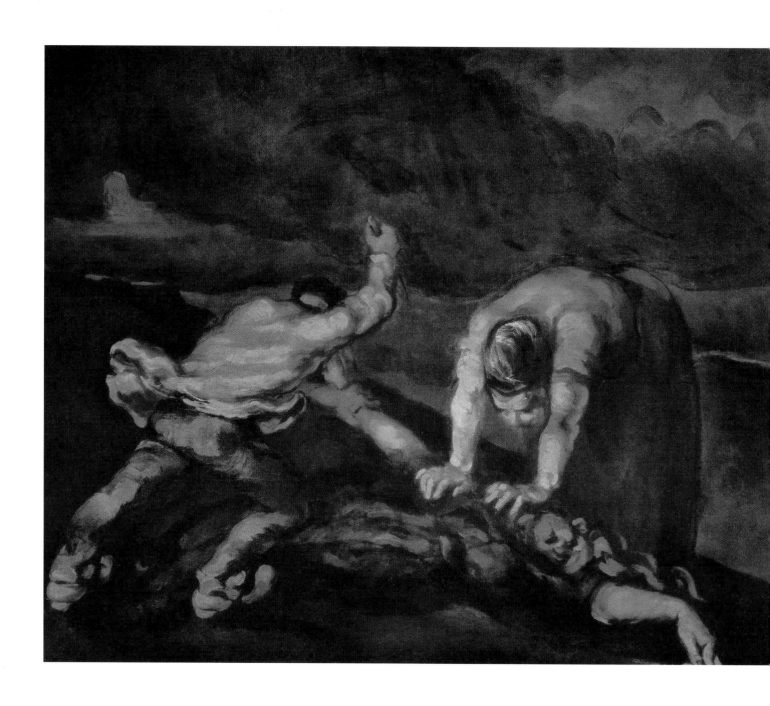

18. *The Murder*,
1867-1870. Walker Art
Gallery, Liverpool.

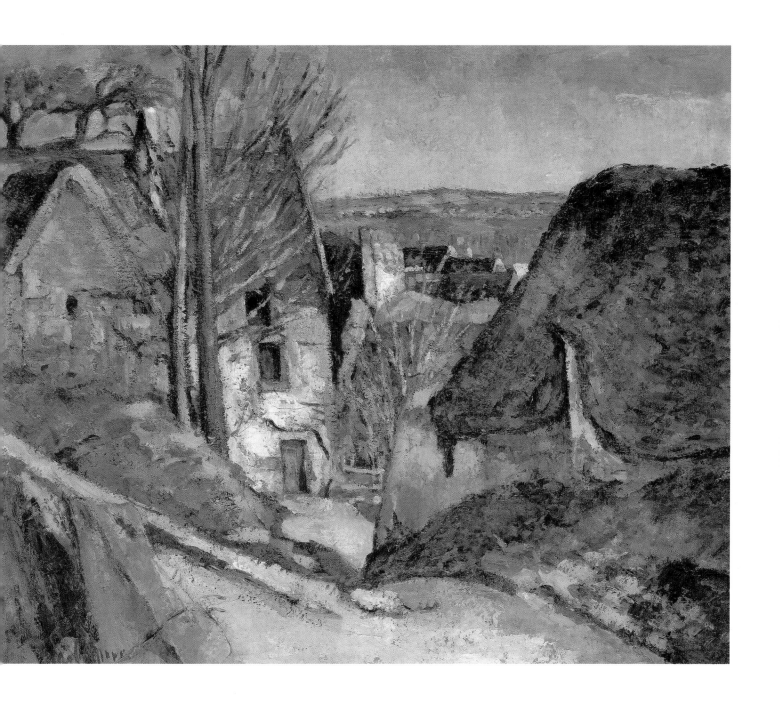

19. ***The House of the
Hanged Man***, 1873.
Musée d'Orsay, Paris.

The titles of these pictures are so out of keeping with the traditional idea of the genre that the painter must have chosen them with tongue in cheek. It can be said without fear of error that despite the many influences apparent in these paintings, they are unique in French mid-nineteenth-century art, being the product of the artist's powerful individual vision of the world.

The painting *Uncle Dominic as a Monk* (c. 1865, Ira Haupt collection New York)(p.12) is one of the *Uncle Dominic* series in which the subject is portrayed in one case as a lawyer, in another wearing ordinary indoor clothes, in others in a cap (p.13) or in fantastic headgear. From the frontal pose in each of these works one can infer that the artist attempted to build up a strongly pronounced relief on the canvas's surface. By piling up dabs of paint one upon the other, he created an almost sculptural effect. Obviously, from the very beginning, Cézanne developed a taste for strongly expressed volume, and his painting *Dish of Peaches* (1860–64) — a copy of part of a composition by a seventeenth-century Dutch still-life artist, displayed in the Aix municipal museum — may serve as an example.
The interest in the interaction of immobility and movement is also evident in the portrait of the artist's father (1866–67, private collection, Paris). By slightly moving the figure in relation to the armchair, and the armchair in relation to the wall, the painter has brought all the elements of the picture into a state of instability which, however, is compensated for by the frontal pose of the figure and the implanting of a large newspaper in the hands of Auguste Cézanne.

Girl at the Piano (1868–69)(p.16) is another, more complex work, and the third and only surviving version of *Overture to 'Tannhäuser'* (1866), so called in tribute to Richard Wagner. The idea of fusing the everyday world with a more elevated one is embodied in the monumental immobility of the figures, the solemn, concentrated calm of their poses, and the measured rhythm of the ornamental pattern calling to mind a musical note or a bass clef as it slowly drifts across the wall.
The compositional scheme worked out by the artist lends the scene a special austerity, uniting all the elements and introducing a note of solemnity comparable to that found in medieval icons. Looking at this canvas, one is aware of Cézanne's immense influence on twentieth-century artists. For the free reconstruction of traditional spatial forms, the violation of established scales, and a synthesized, simplified drawing at which Cézanne arrived by dint of strenuous and intensive experimentation have become a matter of course in twentieth-century art.

20. *Melting Snow at L'Estaque*, ca. 1870. Wildenstein Collection, New York.

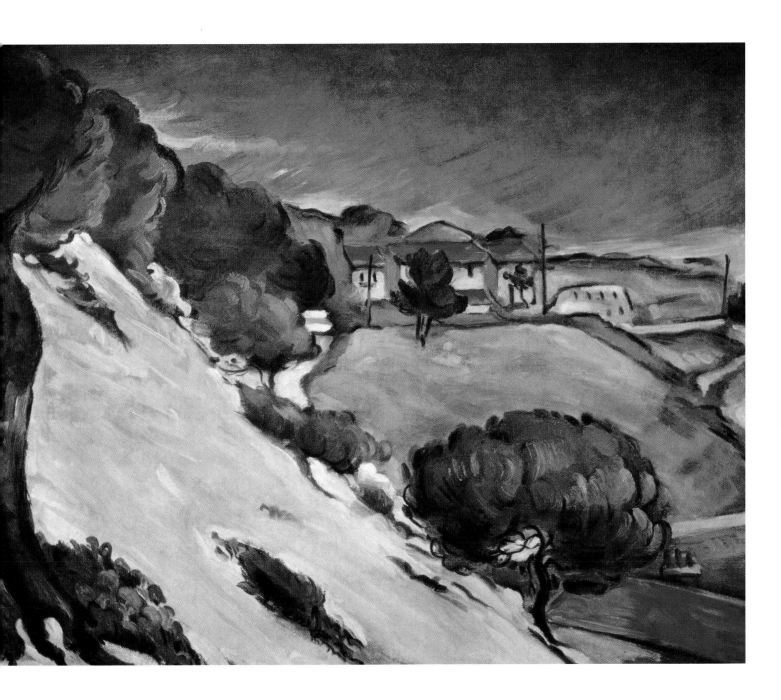

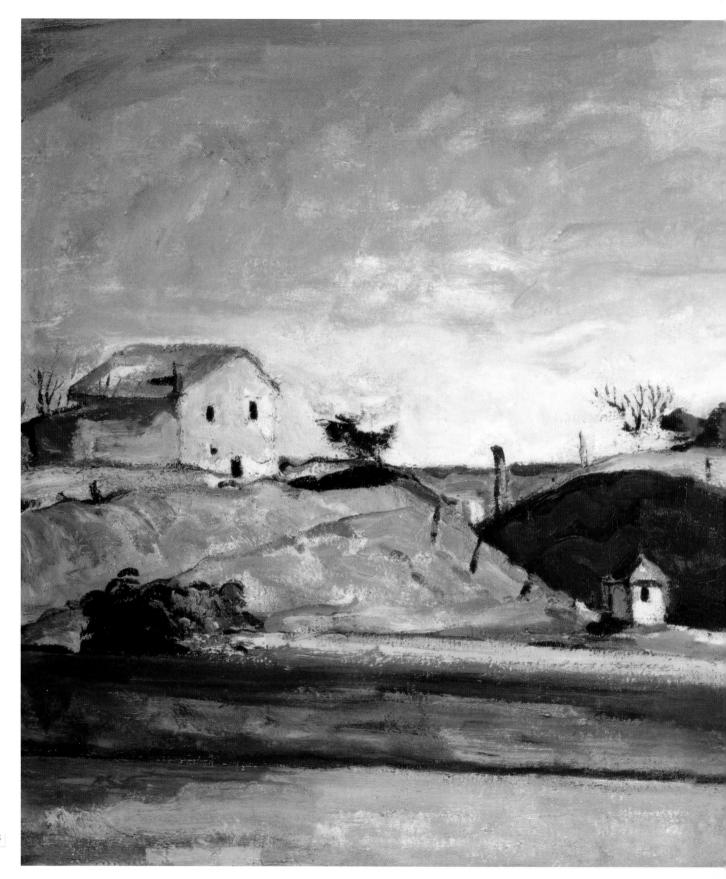

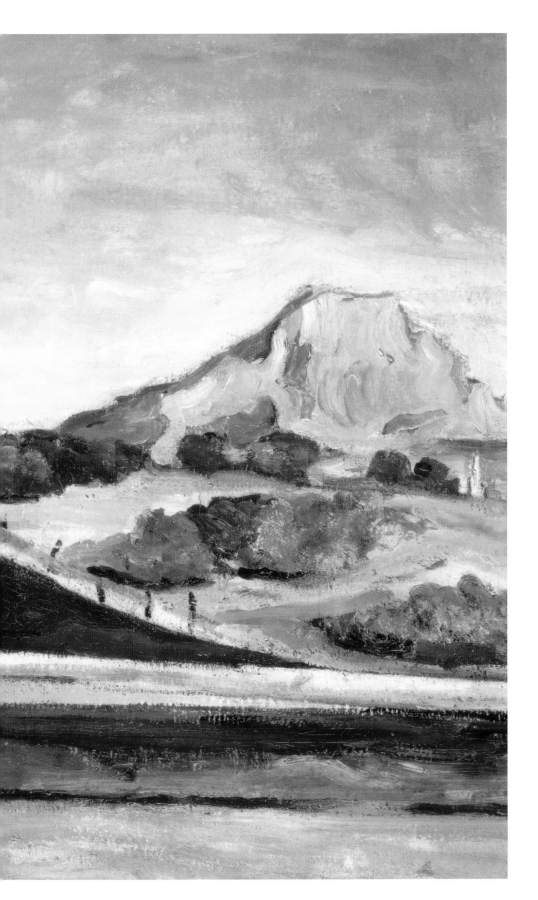

21. ***The Trench and Mont
    Sainte-Victoire*,**
    1870-1871.
    Neue Staatsgalerie,
    Munich.

This and a number of other features give Cézanne's work its originality, make it unlike anything done before his time. But Cézanne fully realized the need of mastering the light-and-air medium and to this end was prepared to forego some of his discoveries. That was one of the reasons why he became close to the Impressionists in the 1870s. Evidence of his first sorties into the outside world is to be seen in his landscapes of the very end of the 1860s. Only in 1872 did he set out to work regularly in the open air.

It may be assumed that Pissarro gave some advice to Cézanne, when he settled in Pontoise in 1872 and when a close creative association came into being between the two painters, which continued with minor breaks until 1877. This was the only period of tutelage in Cézanne's life, a period in which he was directly affected by an outside influence, and Pissarro was the only painter of that time who exercised such an influence upon him. They worked side by side on the same motifs, and certain of their pictures of those years bear traces of mutual influence.

Later Pissarro wrote: " Of course, we were always together; but it is also true that each of us preserved one valuable thing — his own sensation."[5] The first result of this association was a lightening of Cézanne's palette. In his canvas *The House of the Hanged Man at Auvers* (1873, Musée d'Orsay, Paris)(p.25), the only trace of romanticism was the name which, however, had no direct connection with its subject matter. While using light Impressionist tones, Cézanne nevertheless applied the paint thickly.

His contact with Pissarro, and through him, with the Impressionists, at a time when the Impressionist trend had reached its zenith, was a turning point in Cézanne's work. Pissarro gave him a method the absence of which he, Cézanne, acutely felt in his early period. But under Cézanne's brush this method produced unexpected results, for the strivings of Cézanne and those of Pissarro were in many ways dissimilar.

Cézanne willingly listened to Pissarro's advice, especially as this mild and patient man had an exceptional gift as a teacher. But at the beginning of his Auvers period Cézanne was not equipped to react so speedily to what he perceived. He was used to pondering over a painting. His thick, heavy brushstrokes were not suitable for expressing fleeting atmospheric nuances. In addition, he was not satisfied with such unconditional dependence on the chromatic range provided by nature. He wanted to find a synthetic solution to all the harmonies offered by nature, and he strove for constructively well-thought-out space in a painting.

22. *Mont Sainte-Victoire*,
1882-1885.
The Pushkin Museum
of Fine Arts, Moscow.

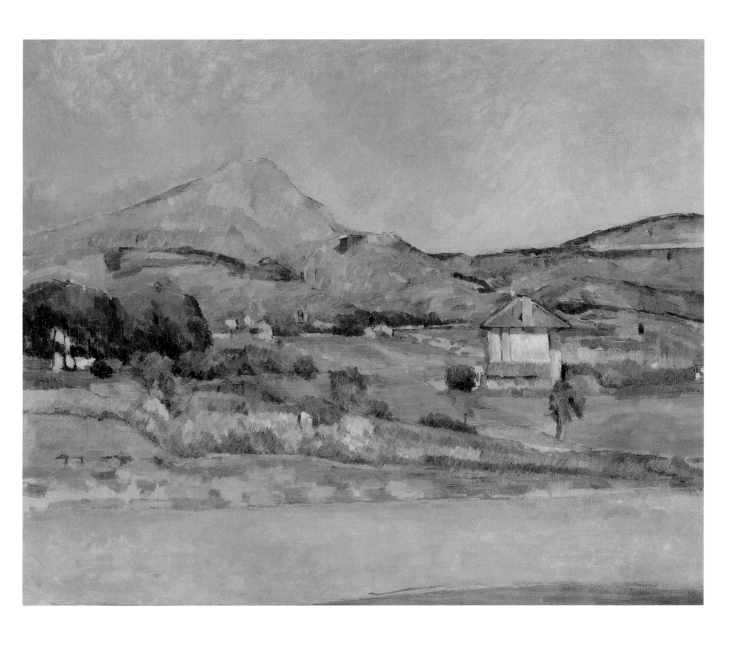

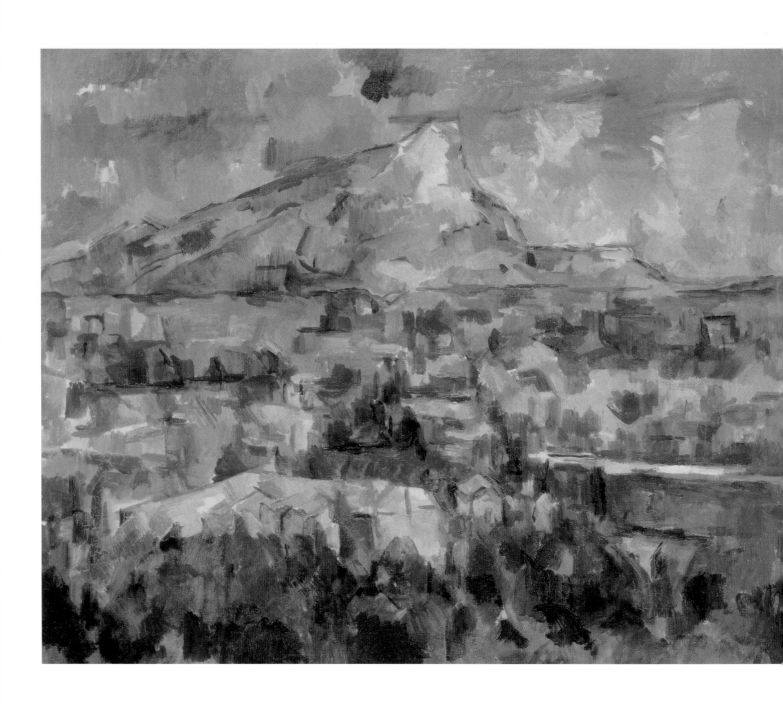

The following dilemma confronted Cézanne: he had either to accept Impressionism with all its wild play of interacting color reflections and shimmering mist of the light-and-air medium, or he must reject it and, together with it, his new perception of the world, a perception that partly under the influence of Impressionism was becoming wider, more profound and more acute. Cézanne wavered. But even in his most Impressionistic works he could never accept entirely the system of painting in tiny, divided brushstrokes which enabled Monet and Pissarro to achieve a sense of the continual changes of air and light.

Road at Pontoise (1875–77, Pushkin Museum of Fine Arts)(p.191) is an example of Cézanne's version of Impressionism. Following Pissarro's advice, he regards the motif first of all "from the point of view of form and color," he "does not fix his eye on one point," does not stress the thematically focal point of a composition — all the elements of a landscape are of equal value in his eyes, and he paints them simultaneously, observing at the same time the reflections of colors on everything that surrounds them. The main problem which Cézanne tackled during this period, whether in landscape, portrait, or still life, was how to achieve the wealth of color reflections revealed by light, while preserving a sense of the material mass and form of objects. Two of his paintings in the Hermitage demonstrate his searchings along these lines, notably *Flowers in a Blue Vase* (p.20) and *Self-Portrait in a Cap* (both done between 1873 and 1875)(p.21).

In his *Flowers in a Blue Vase*, Cézanne brings out the form of the objects by his control of the brush. For Cézanne the bouquet is a combination of separate flowers, stems, and leaves. It is first of all a pictorial form, as strict and definite as the very vessel in which it is held. In *Self-Portrait in a Cap*, the face, the clothes, and the cap are treated as a solid color mass of the same texture throughout. Brushstrokes that are close in tone fuse together to form a single reddish-brown surface on which the green reflections (graduating to violet bluish and blue) create the sensation of natural hollows and recesses filled in with shadow.
The difference between Cézanne's and Pissarro's methods was inelegantly but precisely defined by a peasant who watched both artists at work: "Monsieur Pissarro, when he is working, pokes, Monsieur Cézanne dabs."

The period of Cézanne's closest links with the Impressionists is in the 1870s; he exhibited with them in 1874 and in 1877.

23. *Mont Sainte-Victoire*, 1883-1890. Musée d'Orsay, Paris.

However, by the end of the decade, the artist began to sharply feel the incompatibility of his understanding of a painting with some aspects of the Impressionist method. "I keep on working, but with little success, and it's all too far removed from the general trend…"[6] he wrote in 1878. Cézanne gradually moved away from Impressionism, though continued to be on friendly terms with Monet and Pissarro, even going so far as to work with Renoir in the 1880s, but this time on a new basis.

Thus, at the end of the 1870s, now almost forty, Cézanne once again finds himself at a crossroads. And the painter sets out on a new quest. Strictly speaking, Cézanne's work falls into two main stages: before 1873 and afterwards, when the artist started to paint from life and began to master reality, a process which went on day by day until his very death. Cézanne himself formulated his understanding of theory as *tout est en art surtout théorie, développée et appliquée au contact de la nature.*[7] In other words, for him theory was what Émile Bernard called "thinking with brush in hand" about methods of recreating reality.

Cézanne did not agree with anything less than portraying nature in accordance with truth and "embracing it as a whole." And if perhaps he too often recognized the impossibility of attaining the unattainable, he did not want to reconcile himself to that and could not bring himself to do so.

At a certain stage Cézanne's idea of embracing reality as a whole confronted him with the need to tackle the practical task of maintaining the achievements of the Impressionists, above all in the spatial treatment of light and air, without losing the wealth of objects and colors of reality. Although in the late 1870s Cézanne and the Impressionists parted company, this did not mean an ideological rupture: their aims and tasks continued to coincide in more respects than one.

In his works of the late 1870s, we already see a tendency toward a logical consistency of pictorial means. This becomes especially clear if we compare two self-portraits: one painted in the Impressionist period (1873–75, Hermitage)(p.21) and the other, executed between 1879 and 1885 (Pushkin Museum of Fine Arts)(p.22).

In the Hermitage canvas, Cézanne still makes a substantially intuitive use of the law of optical perception, according to which warm tones (pinks and yellows) seem to stand out, to come nearer to us, and cold ones (blues and greens) recede into the depths. In the Moscow *self-portrait*, these advancing and receding tones are kept under strict, rational control by the artist.

24. *The Jas de Bouffan*, 1885-1887. The Pushkin Museum of Fine Arts, Moscow.

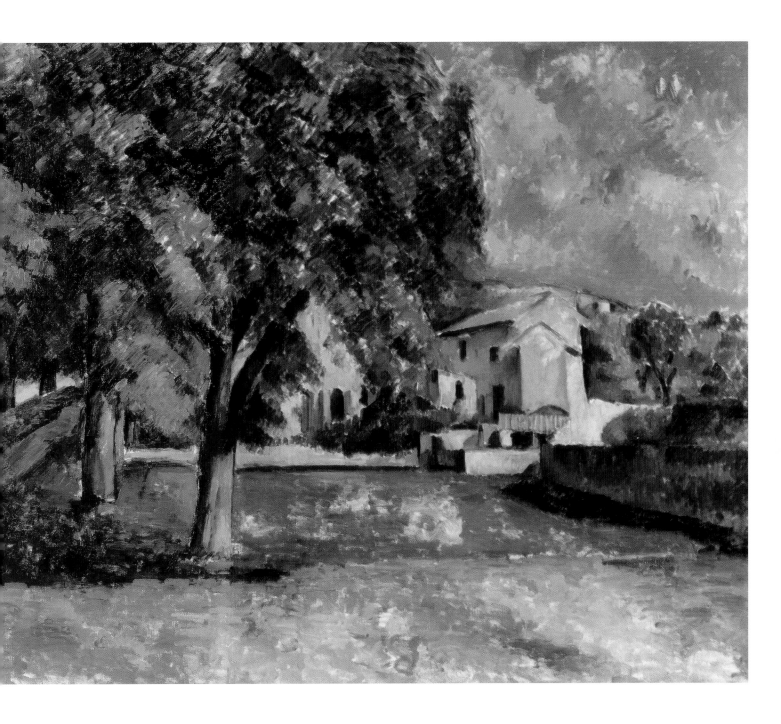

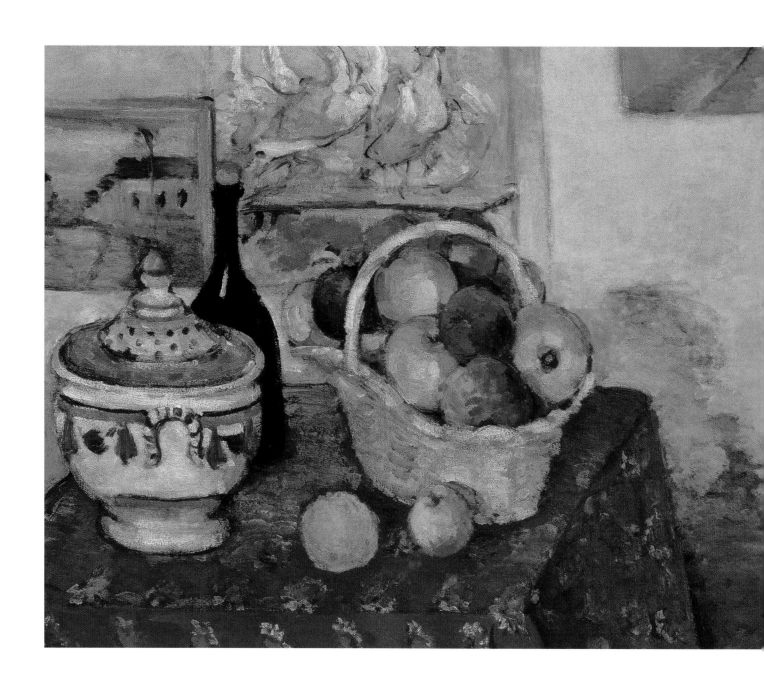

The nearer to the periphery, the thicker their layer, the more intensive their dark cold hues. The nearer to the center, the more warm yellowish tones, gradually changing to yellow, orange, and pink colors, begin to show through. These dabs of paint are not perceived here as color reflections shifting over the surface of the object; they are transformed into certain spatial microplanes used by Cézanne to indicate the extension of form from the surface of the canvas into the depths of the picture.

By this method the artist achieves an almost stereoscopic effect: the left-hand side of the face seems to be illuminated and is therefore approaching us, while the right-hand side is plunged in shade, is receding from us, giving the effect of a turning head. As a result the form takes on a third dimension before our very eyes, demonstrating the unimpeachable logic of its construction.

Perhaps there is no other European artist of the past two centuries in whose work still life has occupied so honored a place. This is quite understandable: Cézanne took up this genre as a result of his heightened interest in plastic form. In the 1880s, he produced numerous variations depicting fruit, crockery, vases, and tablecloths, i.e. everything that was stable and unchanging, that could be painted carefully for a long time.

The still life *Fruit* (c. 1879–80, Hermitage)(p.38) is one of a long series of still lifes of this kind. Here we find the same devices as are seen in the Moscow self-portrait: Cézanne builds up the forms of the objects with the aid of warm, advancing tones and cold, receding color planes. As firm as billiard balls, the orange-colored fruits, press down upon the surface of the table with all their perceptible weight, the yellow lemon acquires three dimensions in the greenish shadows at the edges. At the center of this composition Cézanne places a tablecloth whose soft, amorphous mass does not link the surrounding objects into a single whole but, on the contrary, emphasizes the autonomous existence of each object in pictorial space. The gleaming fruit do not lose their colorfulness in the darkened part of the picture. In this way light ceases to be something external to the object.

Subsequently Cézanne's development proceeds in three main directions, those revealing the rich color relations between objects, the relations between their forms and volumes, and between objects and the space in which they exist. Two still lifes housed in Russian collections, *Peaches and Pears* (1888–90, Pushkin Museum of Fine Arts) and *Still Life with Curtain* (1898–99, Hermitage)(p.72), done ten years later, illustrate the stages along this road.

25. *Still-Life with a Tureen*, ca. 1877. Musée d'Orsay, Paris.

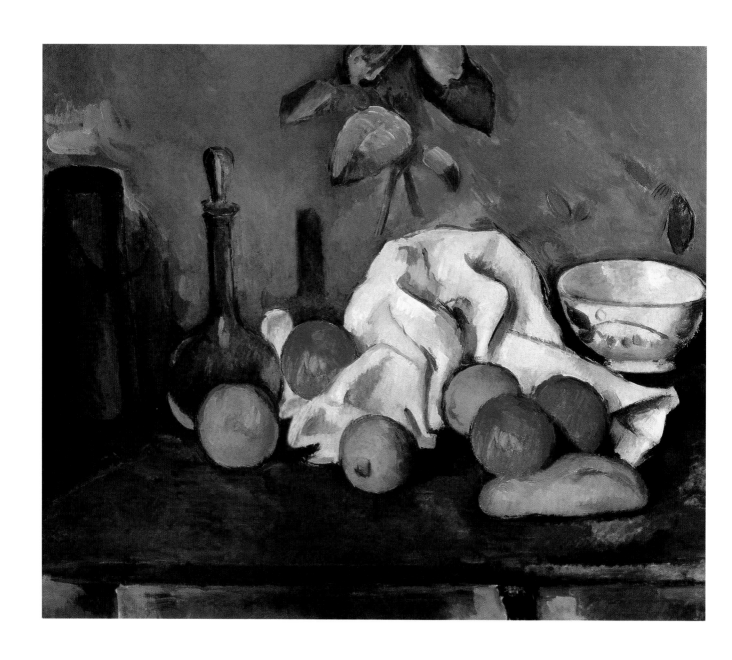

26. *Fruit*, 1879-1882. The
    Hermitage Museum,
    Saint-Petersburg.

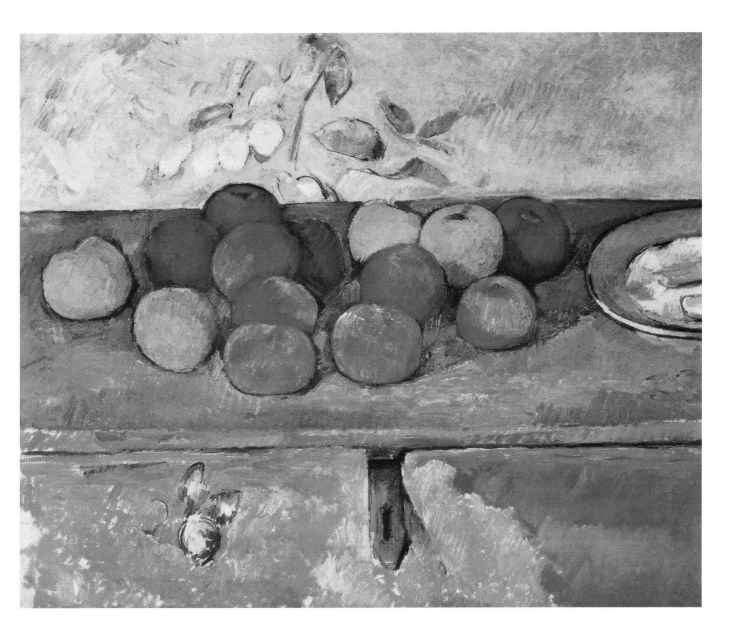

27. ***Apples with a Plate of Biscuits***, 1879-1882.
Musée de l'Orangerie,
Paris.

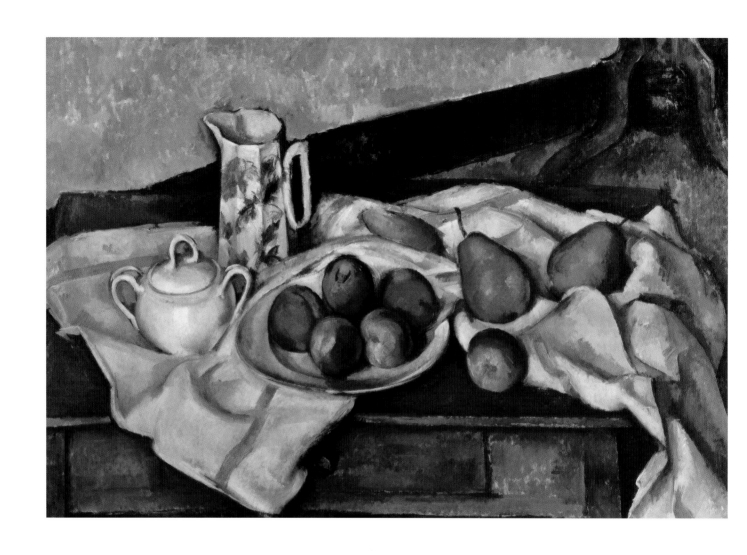

28. *Still-Life*, 1888-1890.
   The Pushkin Museum
   of Fine Arts, Moscow.

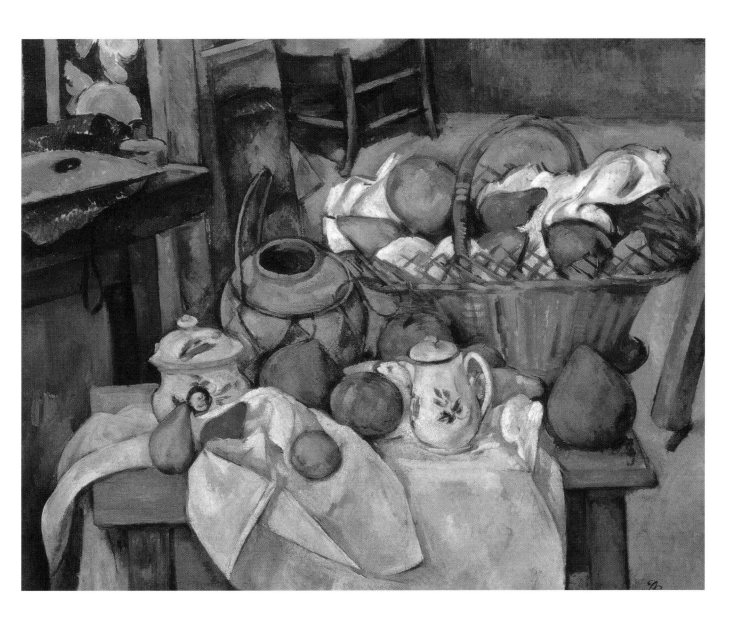

29. ***Still-Life with a
Basket***, 1888-1890.
Musée d'Orsay, Paris.

In comparison with *Fruit*, where the contrast between dark and light parts of the composition still plays a rather significant role, in the *Peaches and Pears*, light has not only ceased to exist as an external source, it has been transformed into the objects' natural color. In handling pictorial space Cézanne does not reject the principles of classical composition based on singling out the central point and arranging the parts in an equilibrium bordering on symmetry. He merely makes these principles more complex, transforms them. The strict order and the complex equilibrium so typical of Cézanne's constructivist period, a period that came to an end about 1890, reign in this painting. One gets quite a different impression from the *Still Life with Curtain* (p.72) kept in the permanent collection of the Hermitage. The dishes of fruit are pushed to the side of the viewer, the fruit hang onto the sloping surface by a miracle governed by the laws of pictorial gravity, obviously in contrast to those of Newton.

The still life, in which the artist could freely arrange objects, was for him a kind of laboratory in handling space. But how can one achieve such integrity in landscape, when the painter, working in the open air, is dependent upon a given space?
This problem must have constantly confronted Cézanne. Its complexity was aggravated by the fact that the artist, relying on the visual authenticity of his perception, also tried to express the all- encompassing, synthetic picture of nature that would accord with his keen sense of the world's great cosmic forces. "One is neither too scrupulous nor too sincere nor too submissive to nature; but one is more or less master of one's model and, above all, of the means of expression. Get to the heart of what is before you and continue to express yourself as logically as possible."[8]: This simple truth expounded by Cézanne was one he scrupulously followed.
Landscape always occupied a prominent place in Cézanne's work. But it was only in 1870–71, during his pre-Impressionist period, when for the first time he turned to the images of L'Estaque and Mont Sainte-Victoire at Aix, that the first signs of a new orientation appeared in his landscapes. *Melting Snow at L'Estaque* (Wildenstein collection, New York)(p.27) and *Trench at the Foot of Mont Sainte-Victoire* (Neue Pinakothek, Munich) are some paintings in which two types of Cézanne's landscape compositions can be discerned — the "baroque," with a dynamic diagonal structure (*Melting Snow at L'Estaque*), and the classical, with an alternation of canvas-wide parallel color zones (*Trench at the Foot of Mont Sainte-Victoire*).
These two canvases are of course merely early experiments; they lack observation of nature and there is no aerial medium what so ever.

30. *View of L'Estaque from the Bay of Marseilles*, 1878-1880. Musée d'Orsay, Paris.

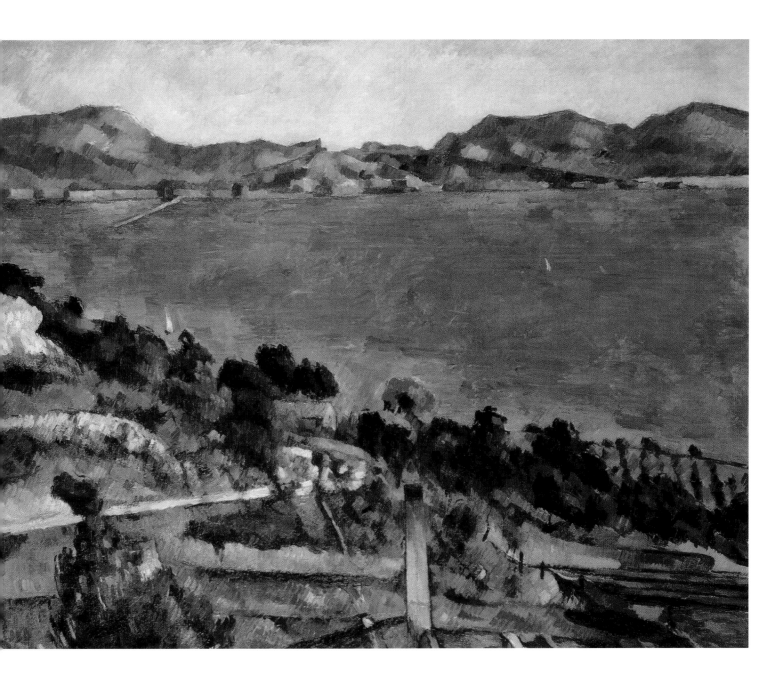

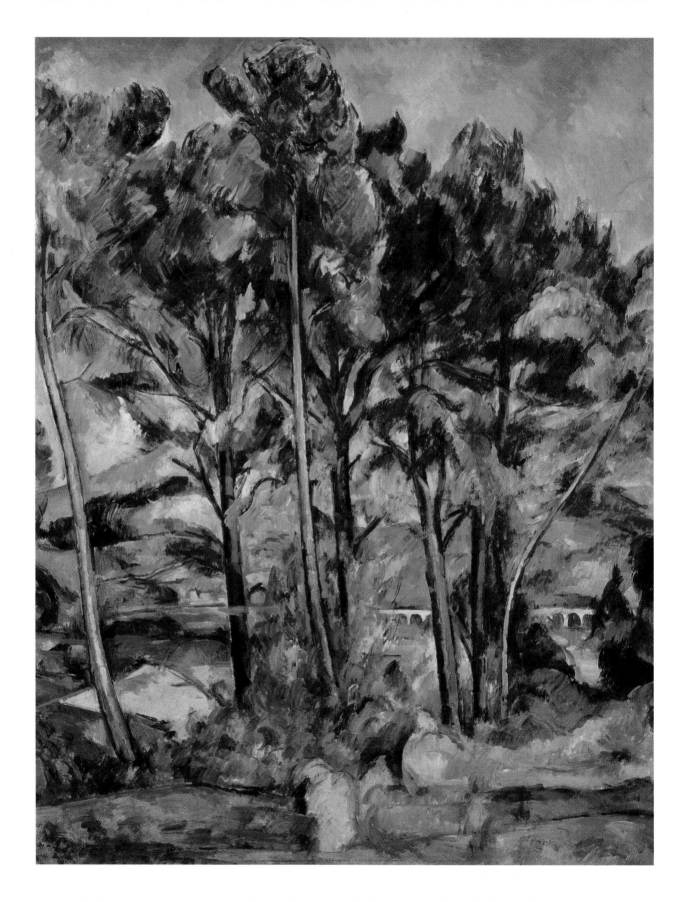

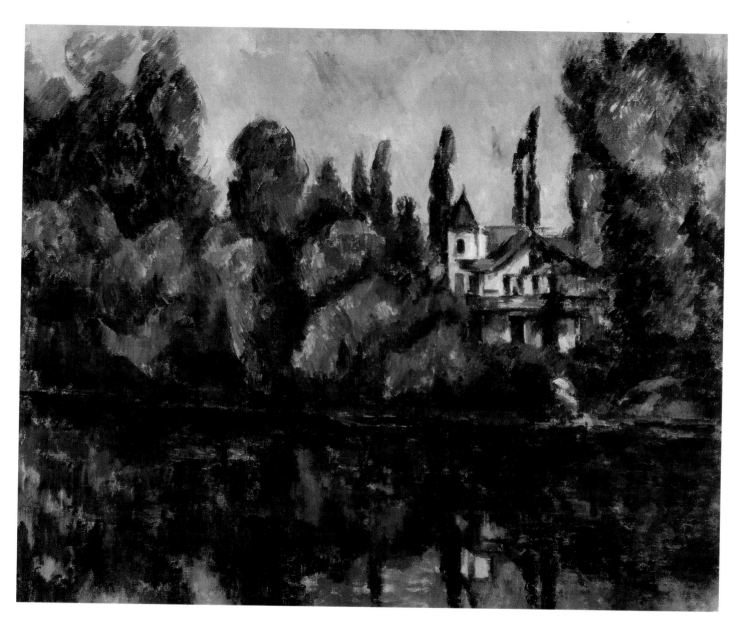

31. **The Aqueduct**,
    1885-1887. The
    Pushkin Museum of
    Fine Arts, Moscow.

32. **The Banks of the
    Marne**, (*Villa on the
    Bank's of a River*),
    1888. The Hermitage
    Museum, St Petersburg.

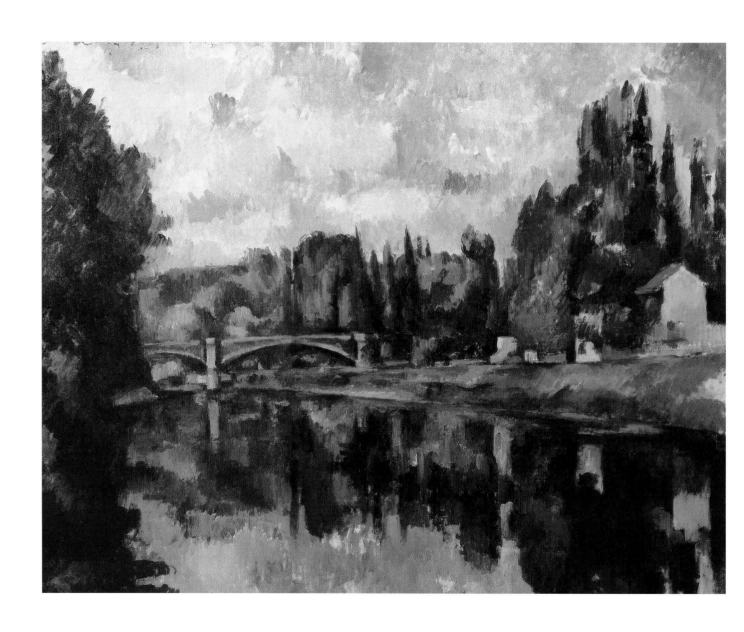

But here one can already see Cézanne's grasp of great spaces and his synthetic image of nature.

Plain by Mont Sainte-Victoire (1882–85, Pushkin Museum of Fine Arts) has some compositional similarity with the *Trench*. But how far the artist has departed from the former image, how complicated space has become in this, at first glance elementary, compositional scheme. The artist leads the viewer's eye to the mountain by means of parallel color zones that imperceptibly taper off into radii.

The compositional scheme of *Trees in a Park* (1885–87, Pushkin Museum of Fine Arts) also has an affinity with the traditional. Nineteenth-century artists often turned to the so-called *sous-bois* method of composition, conveying a sense of depth through a barrier of trees. In *Trees in a Park*, the trees predominate, absorbing into their orbit everything around them. To a certain extent this disguises Cézanne's unconventional understanding of depth. Cézanne reorganizes relations between all objects, violating scale, creating the effect of depth and immediately breaking it down by plunging into inverse perspective. Therefore, objects in the background seem remote and near, and the space of the earth both flat and deep.

From one landscape to another Cézanne experimented in object and spatial relations. In his *Aqueduct* (1885–87, Pushkin Museum of Fine Arts)(p.44), the narrow space of the foreground consists of large green and orange patches, and a row of pines with their boughs raised to the sky is aligned immediately beyond it. But Cézanne eliminates the material differences between spatial planes.

The whirling green brushstrokes model the resilient crowns of the trees, while in the center of the canvas, where the pines cut across the line of the hill on the horizon, these strokes, without losing their specific texture, absorb the bluish-violet tones of the mountain separated from the trees by an immense distance, as if shreds of thickened space, filled with air, are caught between the spreading branches and cannot disengage themselves.

It was in landscapes of this type that the essential aspects of Cézanne's artistic system were realized. In them he shifts planes, intermingles the far and the near, yet preserves a distinct sense of three-dimensionality of space receding into the depths. In this way, and this perhaps is the most important feature, Cézanne consistently avoids indicating the precise place from which he looks at the surrounding environment. It is virtually impossible to define the vantage point from which Cézanne's landscapes were viewed and painted.

33. *The Banks of the Marne River*, 1888. The Pushkin Museum of Fine Arts, Moscow.

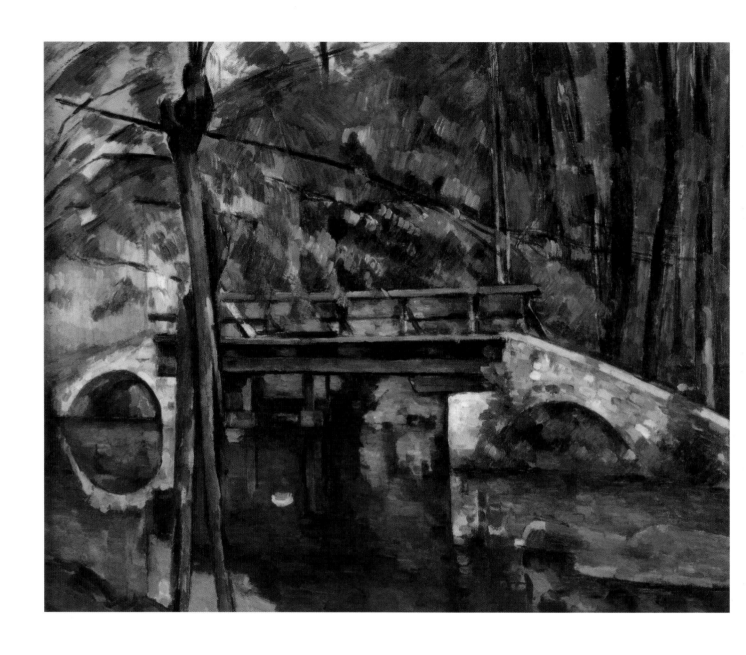

34. ***The Maincy Bridge
Near Melun***, ca. 1879.
Musée d'Orsay, Paris.

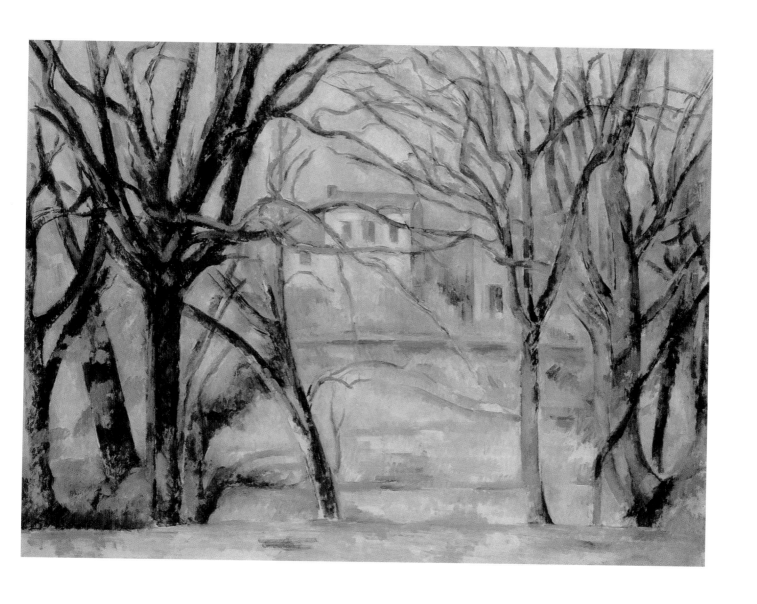

35. *Trees and House*,
1885-1887. Musée
d'Orsay, Paris.

36. *The Bridge*, 1888-
1890. The Pushkin
Museum of Fine Arts,
Moscow.

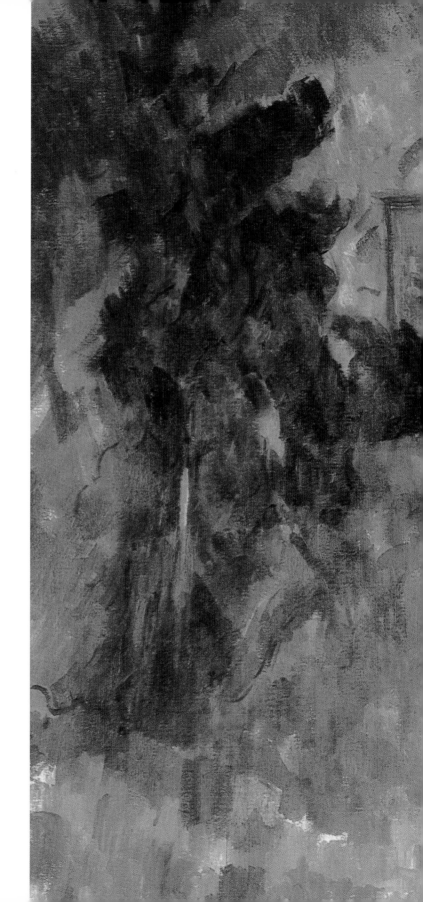

37. ***In the Park of the
    Black Castle***, 1900.
    Musée d'Orsay, Paris.

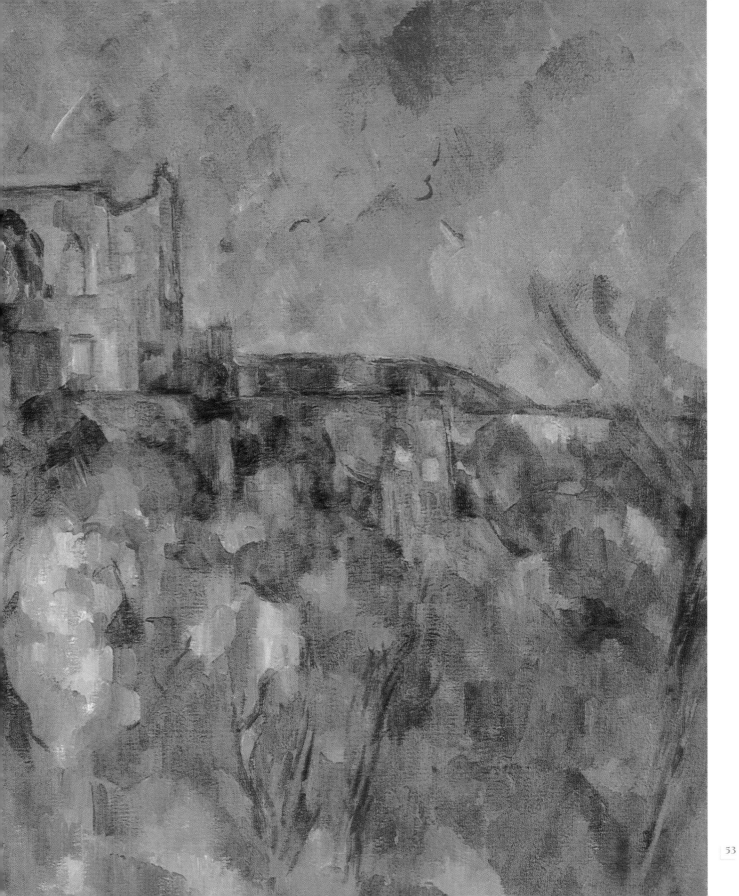

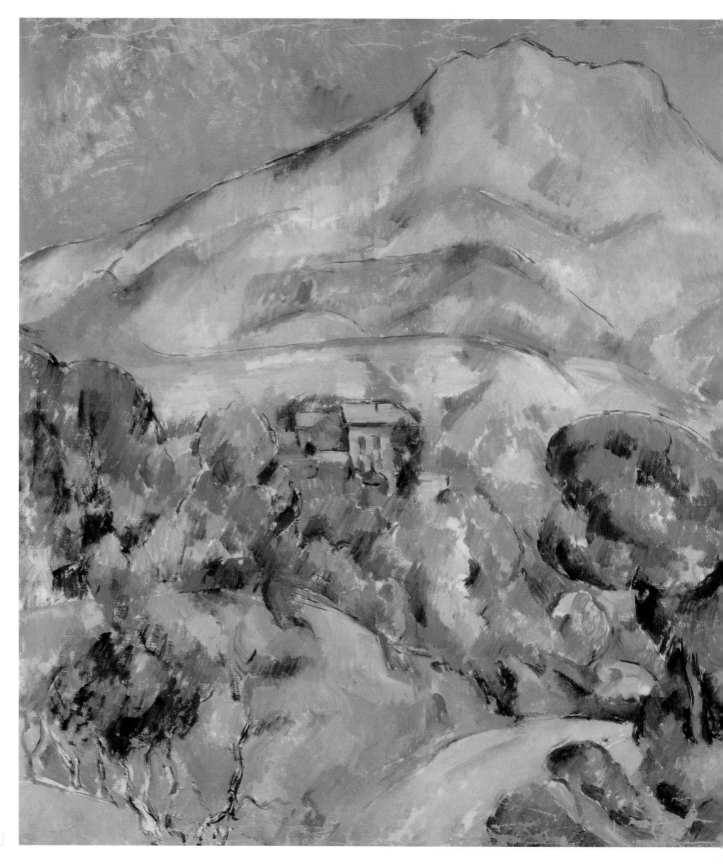

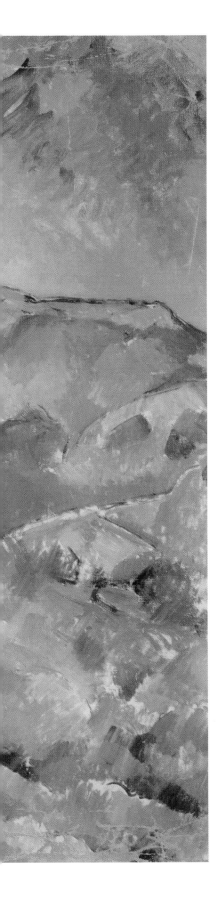

38. *Mont Sainte-Victoire*,
1896-1898.
The Hermitage
Museum,
Saint-Petersburg.

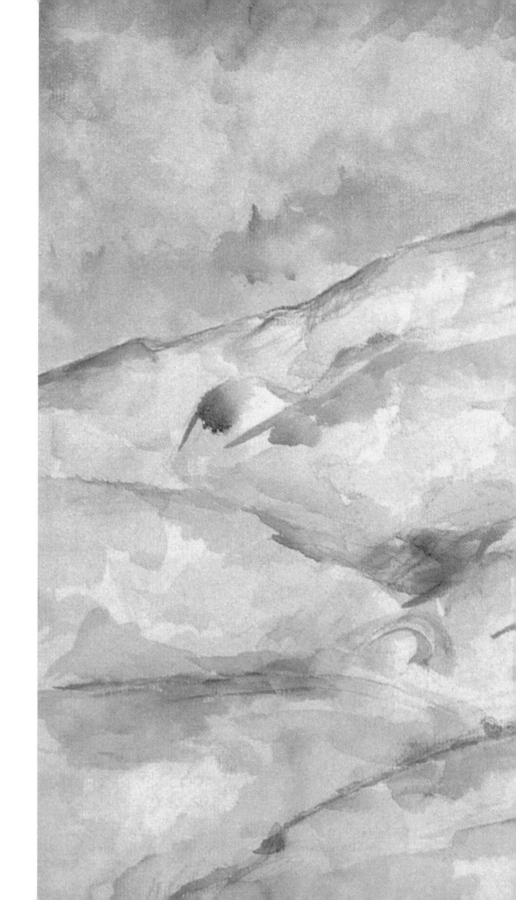

39. *Mont Sainte-Victoire*,
ca. 1900. Musée
d'Orsay, Paris.

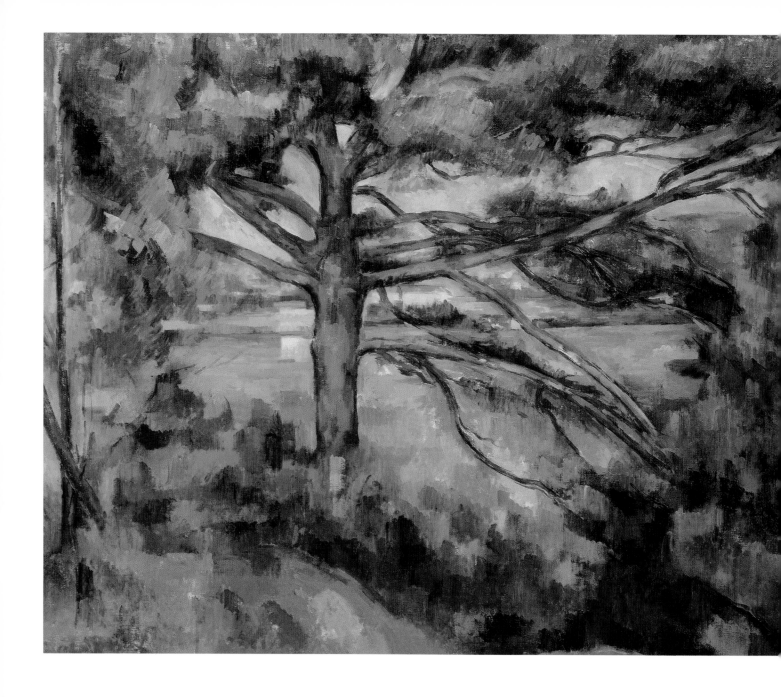

40. *Great Pine Near Aix*,
    late 1890s. The
    Hermitage Museum,
    Saint Petersburg.

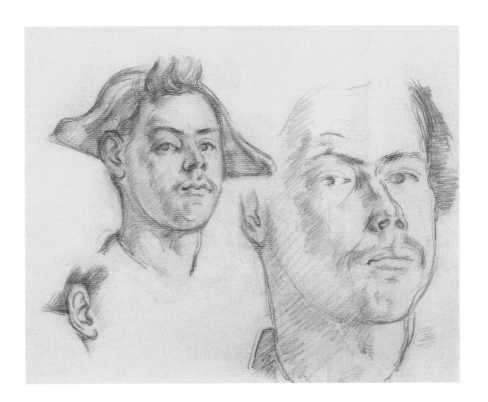

Cézanne's work from the late seventies to the late eighties is usually termed his Constructivist period because of his strictly logical method, rational composition, and so on. These principles determine the style of his portraits, still lifes, and landscapes painted at the time. Perhaps they are most evident in his figure compositions. In 1888, simultaneously with *The Banks of the Marne (Villa on the Bank of a River*, Hermitage)(p.46) Cézanne created another masterpiece, *Pierrot and Harlequin (Mardi Gras)*, in which he depicted the traditional characters of the French folk theater (1888, Pushkin Museum of Fine Arts).

There is no denying that Cézanne's interpretation of the images is traditional, but instead of the usual burlesque clownery, he creates something different. He avoids everything that might seem transient — a spontaneous gesture or fleeting smile. He precludes the slightest possibility of an accidental turn of figure, marking a transition from one movement to another.

In 1886, a change in Cézanne's fortunes occurred. His father died, leaving him the house at Aix, the villa Jas de Bouffan, and a substantial legacy to him and his sisters. Shortly before this Cézanne had married Hortense Fiquet. At last, he was freed of constant financial problems and everyday worries.

41. *Study for the Painting "Shrove Tuesday"*, ca. 1888. Musée d'Orsay, Paris.

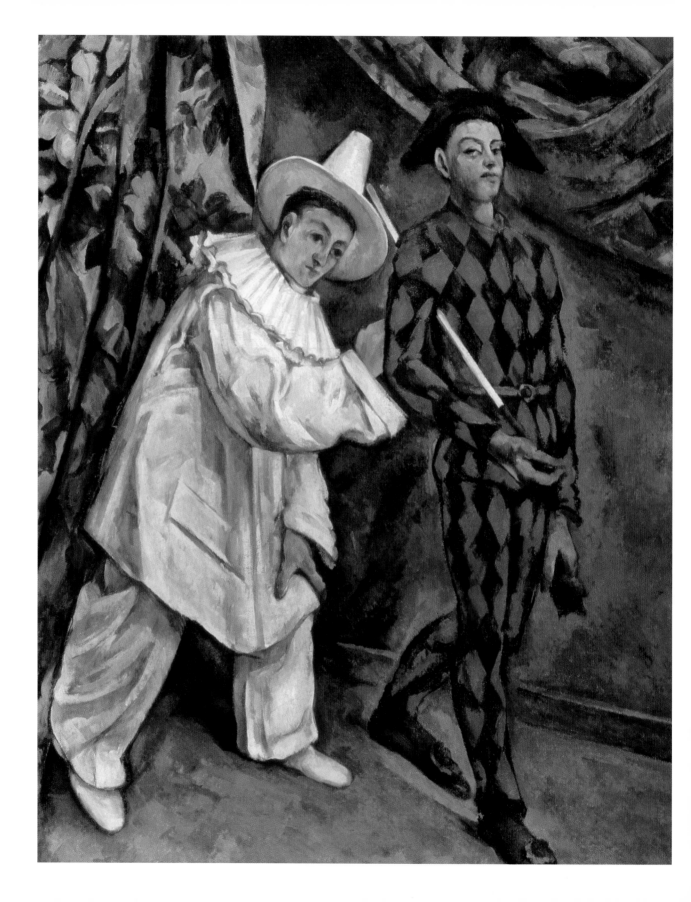

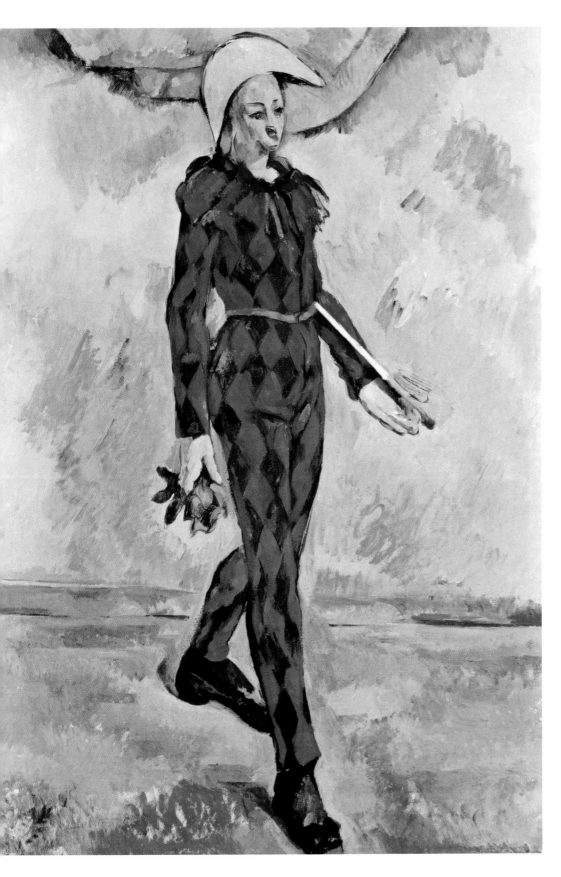

42. **Shrove Tuesday**,
    1888. The Pushkin
    Museum of Fine Arts,
    Moscow.

43. **Harlequin**,
    1889-1890.
    Rotschild Collection,
    Cambridge.

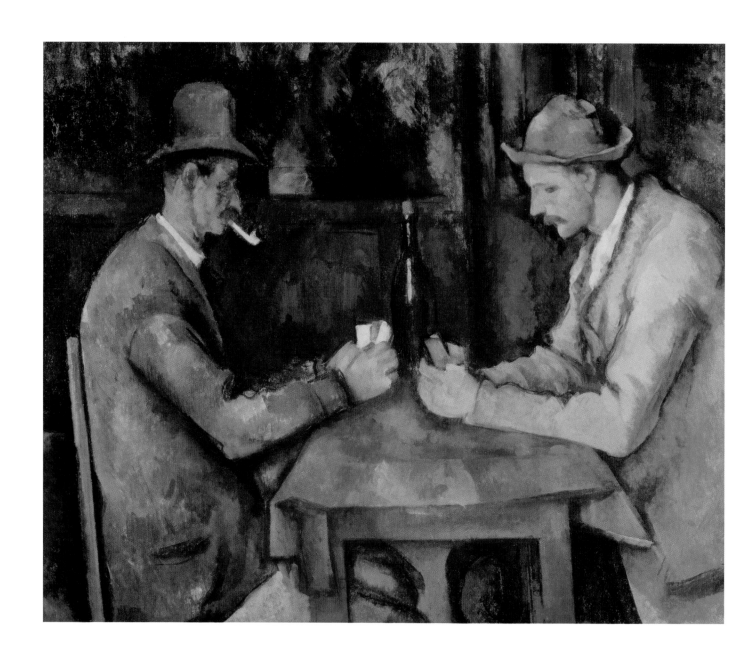

44. *The Card Players*,
    1890-1892. Musée
    d'Orsay, Paris.

Up to that time the jury had only once, in 1882, admitted one of his paintings into the Salon, and that only on the insistence of his friend Antoine Guillemet, while those works which were occasionally displayed at unofficial exhibitions met with furious onslaughts by critics and public alike.

The blows of fate only spurred Cézanne on to harder work. From the beginning of the nineties up to his death he lived almost without a break at Aix, traveling occasionally to Paris to visit his family. Regularly every morning Cézanne would set off to paint. He executed landscapes, portraits, and still lifes. In his studio or at home he painted peasants who posed for him for long periods, retaining throughout their unhurried manner, immobility, and patience — qualities his more intellectual models could seldom attain. This was how he painted his *Card Players* series (1890–92), the finest example of which is in the Musée d'Orsay in Paris. Here two figures and the details of the interior are incorporated into a rigid compositional scheme. If in the mind's eye one prolongs the inclinations of the figures of the two players, and the lines of their hands, then a distinct rhomboid is formed, the apexes of which lie outside the canvas; at the same time the bottle in the center of the composition divides the rhomboid vertically, and the rear edge of the table horizontally. This constructivist logic gives the composition a surprising stability and imparts a monumental quality to the images of the peasants.

Two paintings in Russian collections are executed in the same way: *The Smoker* (Hermitage)(p.65), and *Man Smoking a Pipe* (Pushkin Museum of Fine Arts)(p.64), both dated 1895–1900.

One would have thought that toward the end of the 1880s Cézanne was achieving his desire: he transformed Impressionism into "something solid and durable, like the art of the museums." In place of the fragmentary character of an Impressionist painting, Cézanne asserted the composition structured according to classical laws, in place of the fleeting nature of atmospheric and psychological states came Cézannesque stability, based on an equilibrium between immobility and movement. Evidently, this too could not completely satisfy the artist whose main aim was to "embrace reality as a whole."

In his later years, Cézanne experienced a re-awakening of the sensations of his romantic youth — sensations of the intense and dynamic life of the universe. To him the realization of this meant the coupling of one more, and now last, link to his system of embodying reality; it meant setting down on the immobile surface of the canvas the motion of formative rhythms and processes of life as they come into being, at the same time preserving the material stability of natural forms.

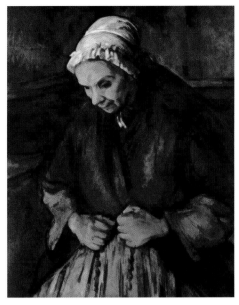

45. ***The Old Lady with a Rosary***, 1900-1904. The National Gallery, London.

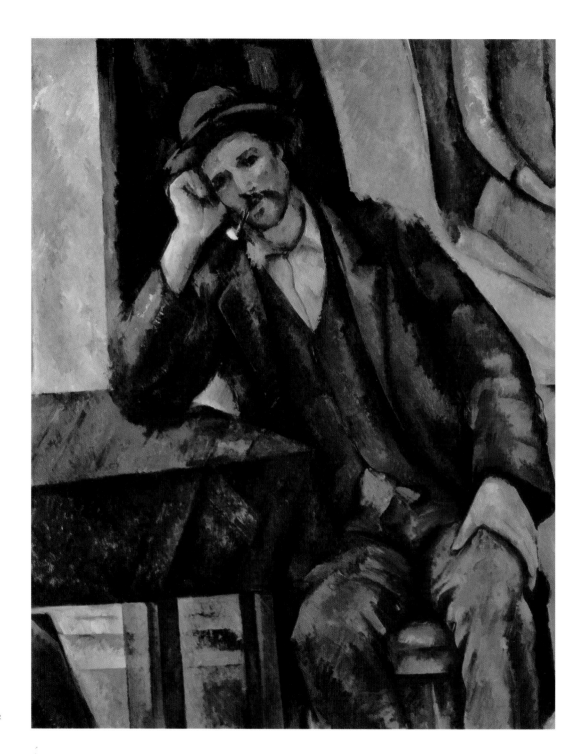

46. *Man Smoking a Pipe*, 1895–1900. The Pushkin Museum of Fine Arts, Moscow.

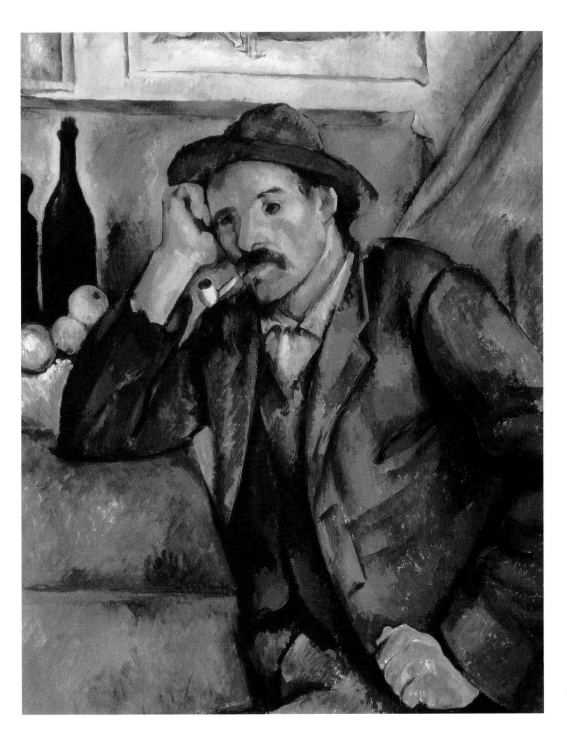

47. ***The Smoker***,
1895-1900. The
Hermitage Museum,
Saint-Petersburg.

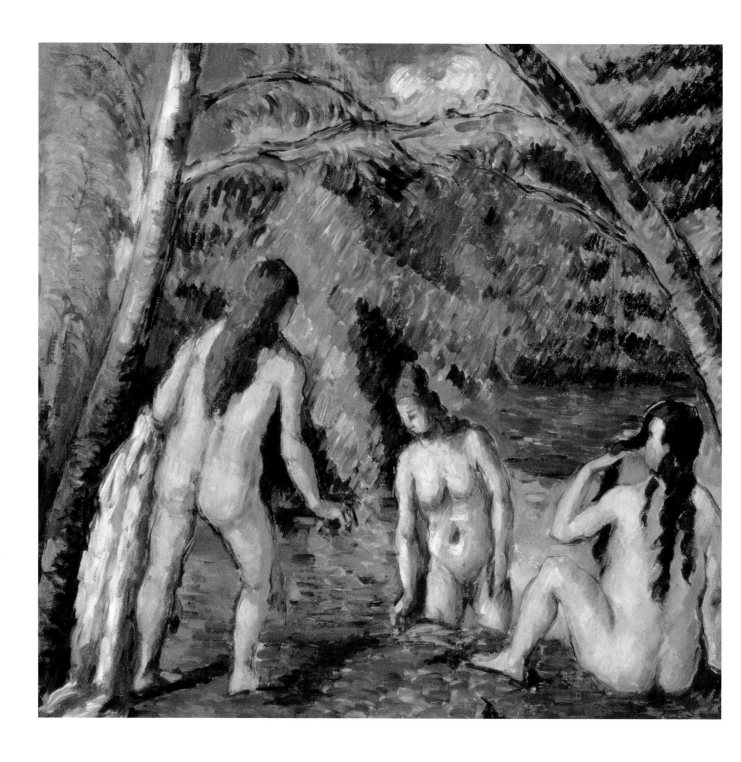

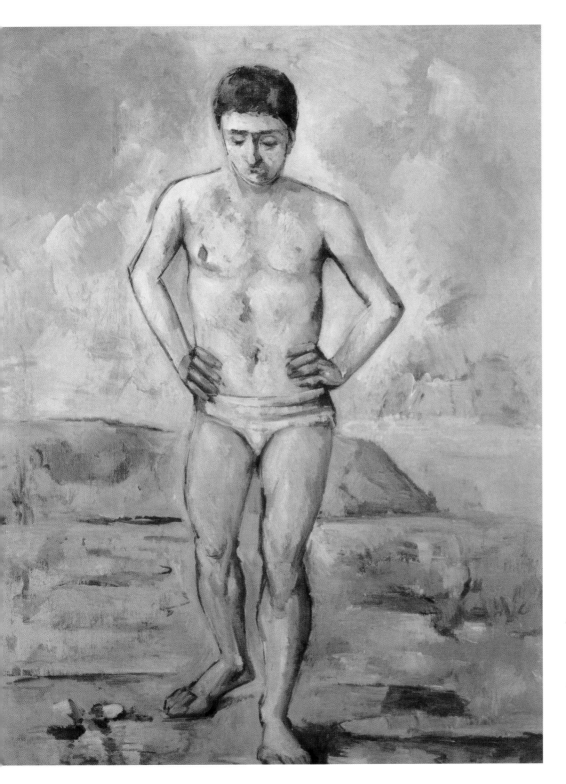

48. *Three Bathers*,
    1875-1877. Musée du
    Petit Palais, Paris.

49. *The Great Bather*, ca.
    1885. The Museum of
    Modern Art,
    New York.

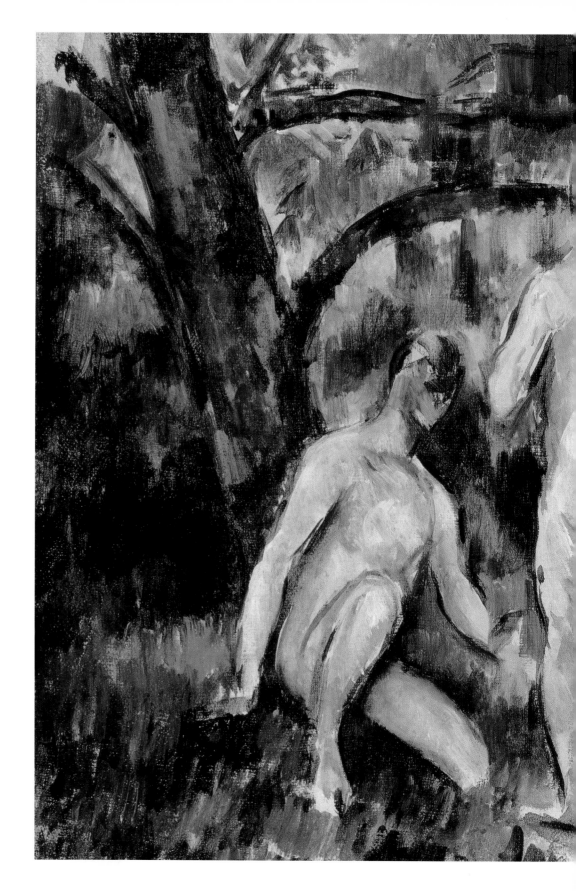

50. *Study of Bathers*,
early 1890s. The
Pushkin Museum of
Fine Arts Museum,
Moscow.

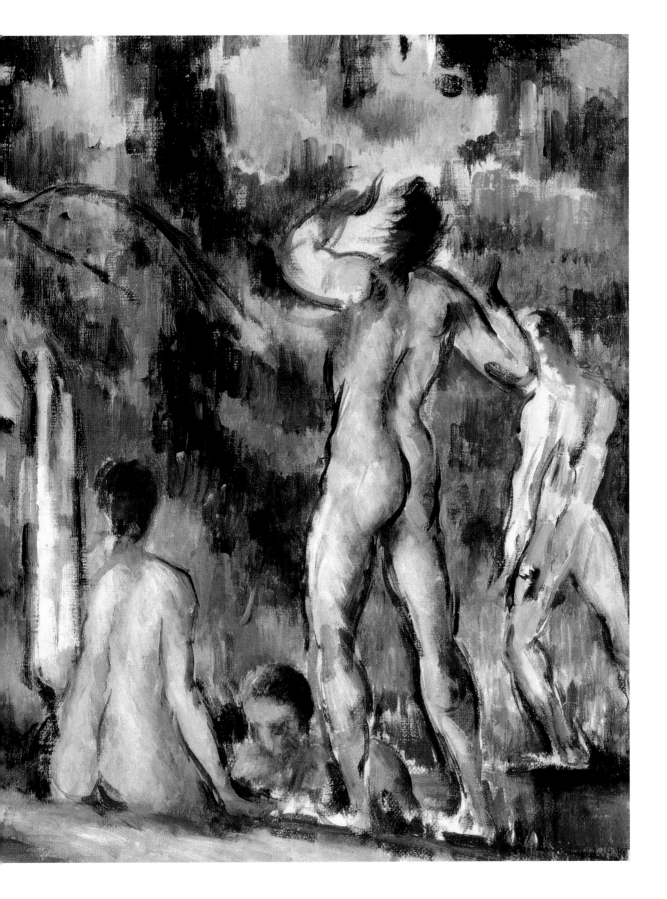

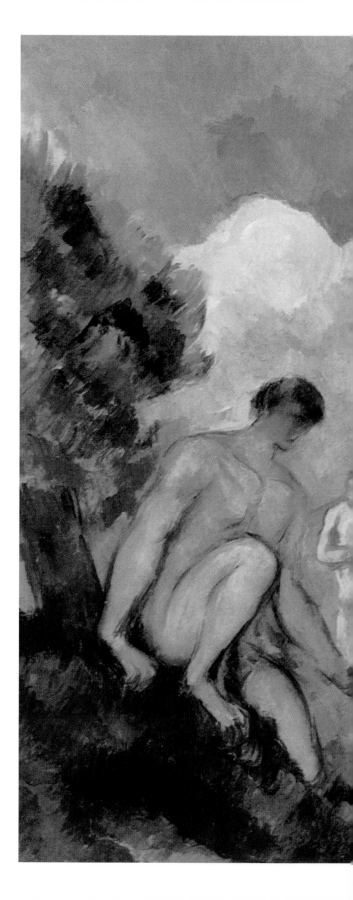

51. *The Bathers*, ca.
1895. Musée d'Orsay,
Paris.

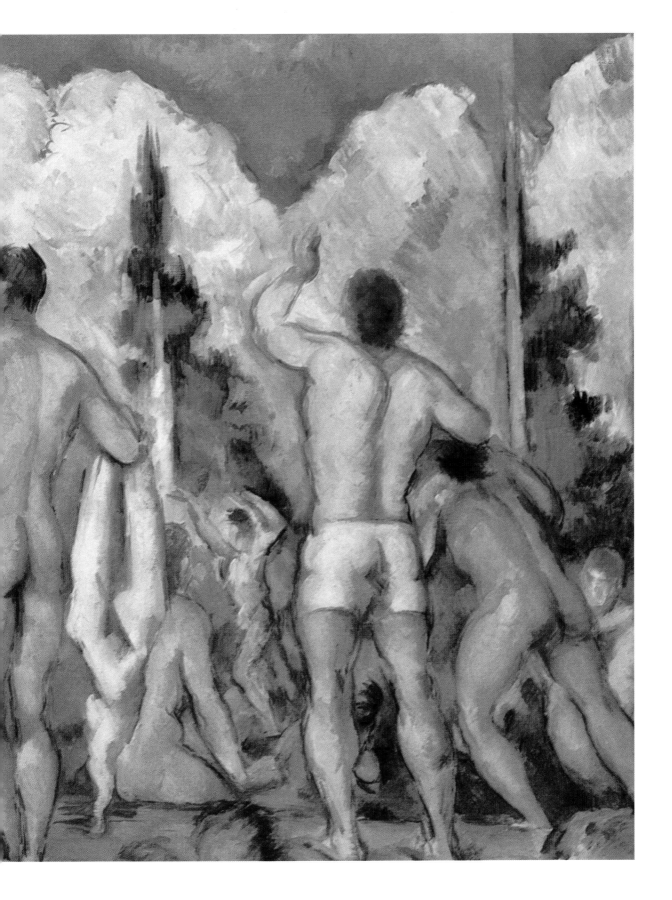

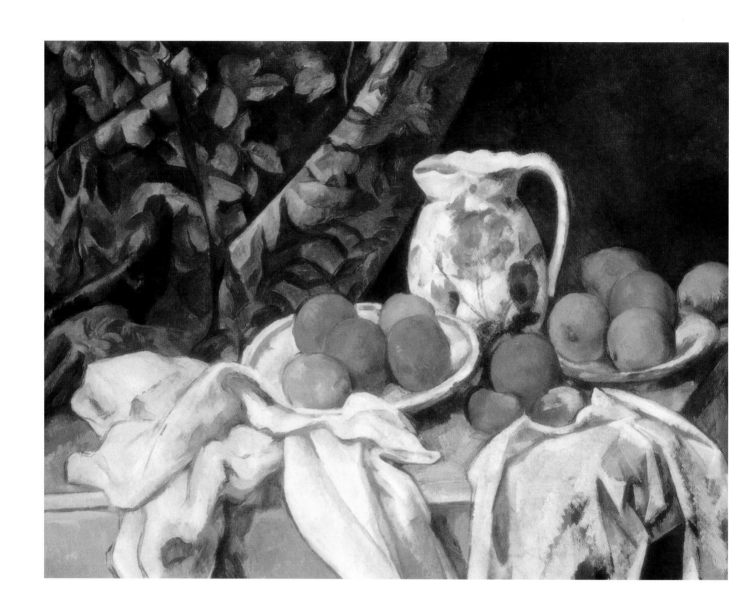

52. ***Still-Life with
    Curtain***, 1898-1899.
    The Hermitage
    Museum,
    Saint-Petersburg.

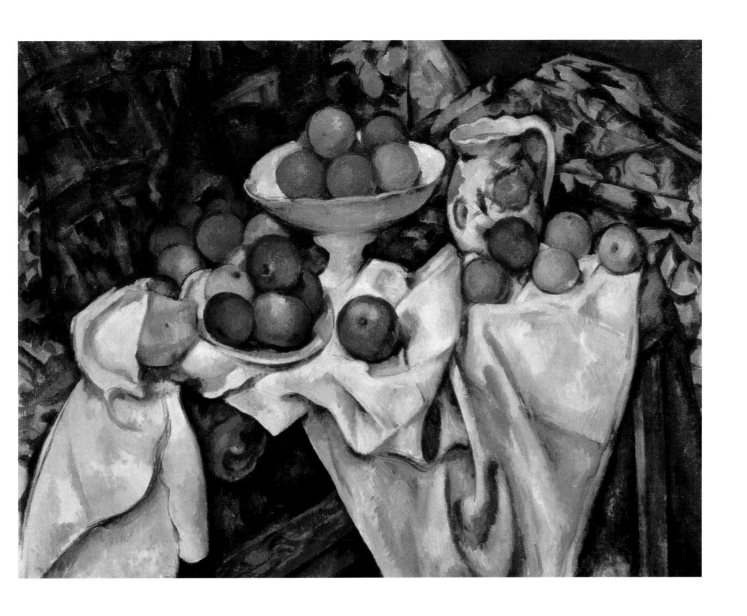

53. *Apples and Oranges*,
1898-1899. Musée
d'Orsay, Paris.

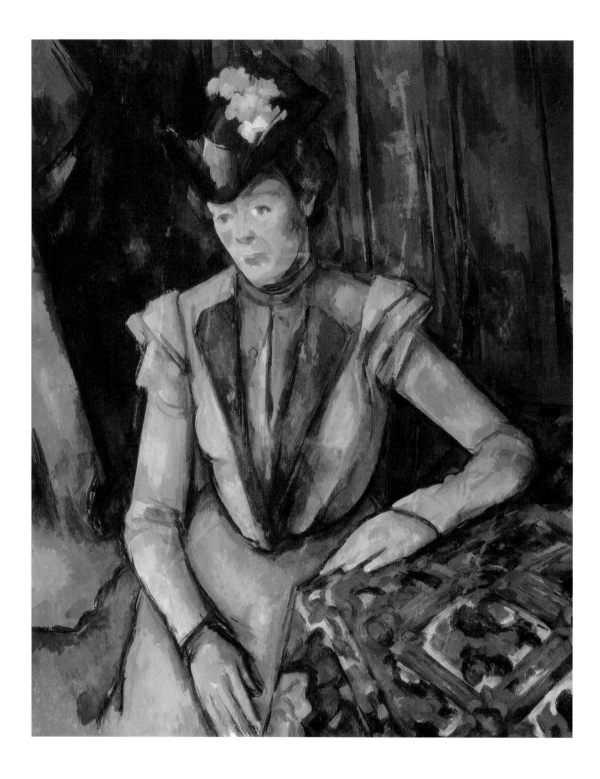

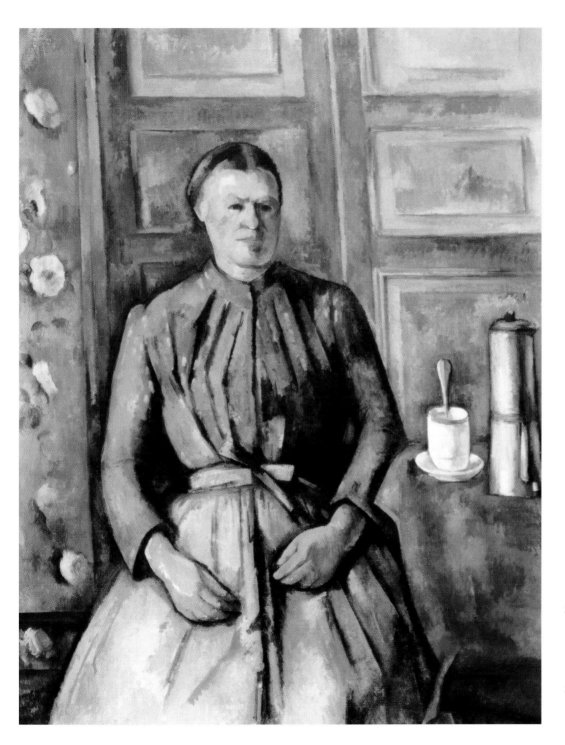

54. ***The Lady in Blue***,
   1898-1899. The
   Hermitage Museum,
   Saint Petersburg.

55. ***The Lady with a
   Coffee-Pot***,
   1890-1894. Musée
   d'Orsay, Paris.

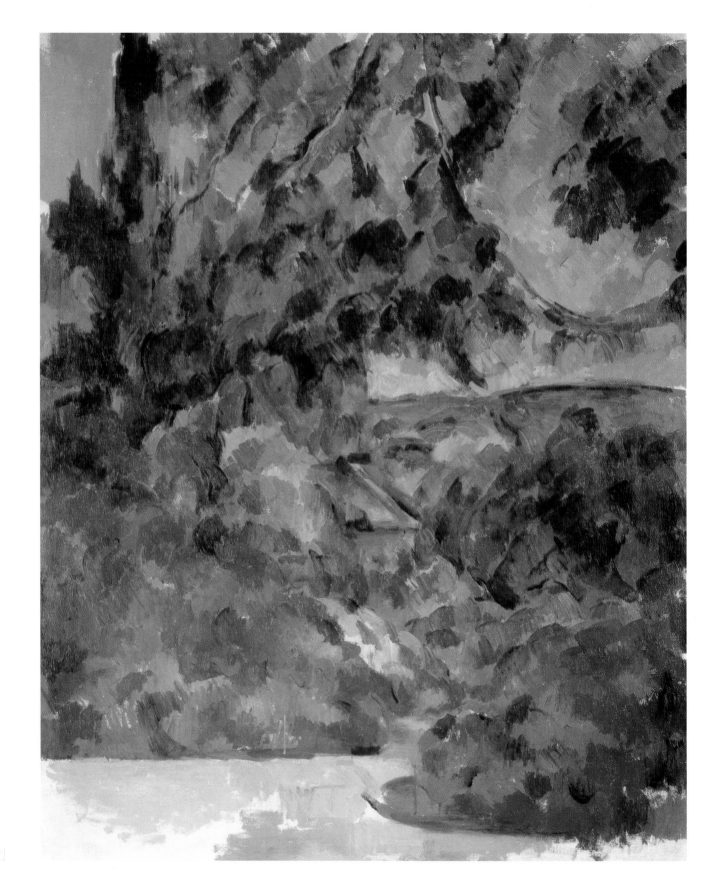

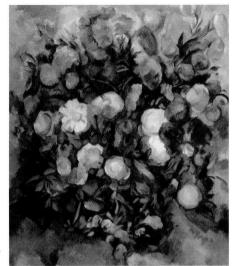

It was a formidable task which necessitated a reassessment of all his old ideas.
One of the supreme achievements of Cézanne's later period is undoubtedly *Mont Sainte-Victoire* (1896–98, Hermitage)(p.54). The dynamic motion permeating this landscape can be sensed both in the movement of the brushstrokes and in the energetic curving of the lines and vibrations of the light-and-air medium.

If one looks at Mont Sainte-Victoire from the side Cézanne painted it, one gets quite a different view from that shown in his painting. Cézanne placed houses which in reality are hidden by trees at the very foot of the mountain; he considerably increased the size of the mountain in comparison with the adjacent hollows and tracts of forest. As a result, though the mountain comes closer to the viewer, there is no loss whatever of the impression of inaccessible distance, like the sensation experienced on looking from a valley at a mountain ridge which seems near and far at the same time.

In his *Great Pine Near Aix* (late 1890s, Hermitage)(p.58), Cézanne was also concerned with developing spherical space.

The tree trunk is framed on all four sides by an uneven ring of color in which the green tones of the pine and the carpet of grass are mixed with bluish-violet reflections of air and distance. Scholars have noted the presence of this "spherical space" in Cézanne's work more than once.[9]

However, claims that Cézanne was the first in this field require a little correction. In his mature years, Cézanne's vision not only became free of symbolic conceptions, but of a host of artistic canons as well. He eventually noticed that in nature all lines bend, curve or incline, and to portray parallels converging in space was to him tantamount to "copying truth from a preconceived type," whereas he wanted "to imitate nature in accordance with truth." To some extent this led to the stories that Cézanne had defective eyesight. Cézanne himself was very near to believing that his sight was defective and ascribed to it the fact that "the planes overlap each other," while "absolutely vertical lines seemed to me to be falling."[10]

56. *The Blue Landscape*,
1904-1906.
The Hermitage
Museum,
Saint-Petersburg.

57. *Study of Flowers*, ca.
1900. The Pushkin
Museum of Fine Arts,
Moscow.

But Cézanne did not want to change his vision of nature and he could not do so. The spherical character of space helped him to convey in the best possible way his pantheistic perception of the dynamic life of nature as a single process uniting and forming in its course all the elements of nature's visual aspect.

One might say that Cézanne's pantheistic world perception was seen earlier in his *Bathers* series in which he tackled the task of uniting human figures with landscapes.

He had turned to this theme back in the 1870s, and had continued with it all through his artistic career. His small study *Bathers* (early 1890s, Pushkin Museum of Fine Arts)(p.68) is part of this series. A group of bathers is depicted on a narrow strip in the foreground, and behind them the color patches of the foliage are interrupted by the light blue patches of sky. But is it the sky? Or is it the wide blue surface of the river, reflecting sky and bank?

In his later landscapes, *Flowers* (c. 1900, Pushkin Museum of Fine Arts) or *Landscape at Aix* (*Mont Sainte-Victoire*) (1905, Pushkin Museum of Fine Arts)(p.79) Cézanne synthesized the principles of organization of pictorial space worked out by him earlier. He was motivated by the same striving to embrace reality as a whole, which now, as ever before, meant for him the fullest possible expression of his sensation of nature. And to achieve this he perfected to the utmost his method of discarding secondary details in order to penetrate the essence of what was portrayed. In these landscapes, nature in many respects loses the concreteness of its forms but acquires instead the dynamic intensity of its existence.

Unlike the Impressionists, Cézanne did not dissolve natural forms in the light-and-air medium; rather he fused them together, and from this alloy, which has absorbed all the colors and shades of reality, he built the world anew. And this process of creation broke off only with his last heartbeat, the last stroke of his brush. Cézanne died on October 22, 1906, from pneumonia, after catching cold while working on his last "motif".

58. *Landscape at Aix* (*Mont Sainte-Victoire*), 1905. The Pushkin Museum of Fine Arts, Moscow.

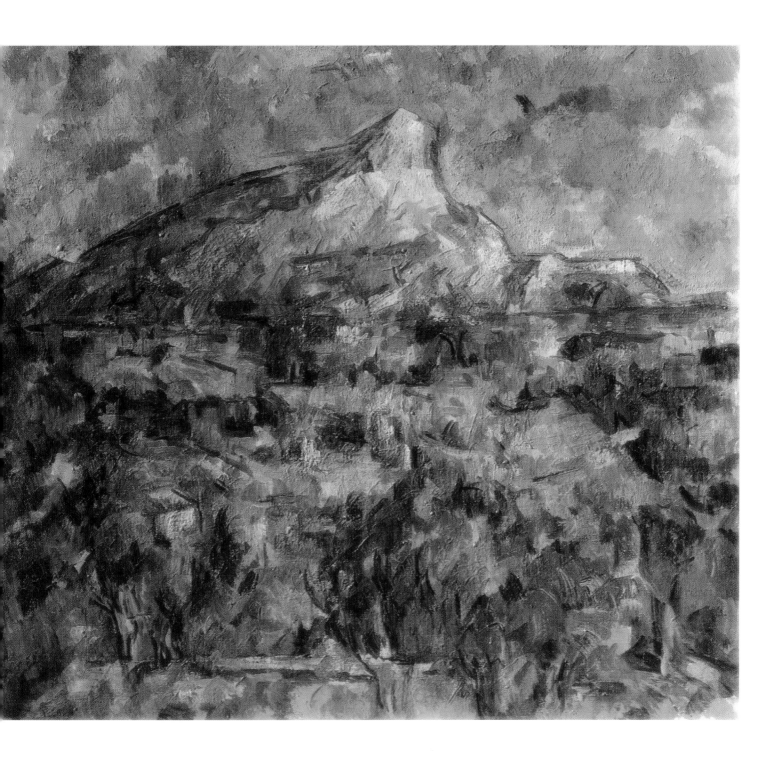

List of Illustrations

Notes

[1] L. Venturi, *Da Manet a Lautrec*, Florence, 1950, p. 107.

[2] A. Nuremberg, *Paul Cézanne*, Moscou, 1926, p. 33

[3] Letter to Numa Coste, February 27, 1864.

[4] Letter to Émile Bernard, September 21, 1906.

[5] Letter from Pissaro to his son Lucien, November 22, 1895.

[6] Letter to Émile Zola, April 14, 1878.

[7] Letter to Charles Camoin, February 22, 1903.

[8] Letter to Émile Bernard, May 26, 1904.

[9] Thus, speaking of Cézanne's landscapes, V. Prokofyev remarks: "The spheroid quality of space in which we have our existence has been made visible for the first time in the history of art." From the epilogue to A. Perruchot, *Cézanne*, Moscow, 1966, p. 351 ff. (in Russian).

[10] Émile Bernard, *op. cit.*, Nos. 247, 248.